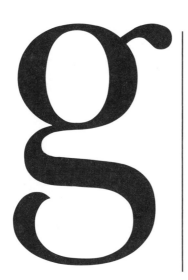

FRACTIONS, DECIMALS, & PERCENTS

Math Strategy Guide

This guide provides an in-depth look at the variety of GMAT questions that test your knowledge of fractions, decimals, and percents. Learn to see the connections among these part–whole relationships and practice implementing strategic shortcuts.

Fractions, Decimals, and Percents GMAT Strategy Guide, Fourth Edition

10–digit International Standard Book Number: 0-9824238-2-9
13–digit International Standard Book Number: 978-0-9824238-2-0

Note: *GMAT, Graduate Management Admission Test, Graduate Management Admission Council,* and *GMAC* are all registered trademarks of the Graduate Management Admission Council which neither sponsors nor is affiliated in any way with this product.

8 GUIDE INSTRUCTIONAL SERIES

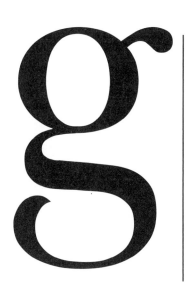

Math GMAT Strategy Guides

Number Properties (ISBN: 978-0-9824238-4-4)

Fractions, Decimals, & Percents (ISBN: 978-0-9824238-2-0)

Equations, Inequalities, & VICs (ISBN: 978-0-9824238-1-3)

Word Translations (ISBN: 978-0-9824238-7-5)

Geometry (ISBN: 978-0-9824238-3-7)

Verbal GMAT Strategy Guides

Critical Reasoning (ISBN: 978-0-9824238-0-6)

Reading Comprehension (ISBN: 978-0-9824238-5-1)

Sentence Correction (ISBN: 978-0-9824238-6-8)

ManhattanGMAT
the new standard

July 1st, 2010

Dear Student,

Thank you for picking up one of the Manhattan GMAT Strategy Guides—we hope that it refreshes your memory of the junior-high math that you haven't used in years. Maybe it will even teach you a new thing or two.

As with most accomplishments, there were many people involved in the various iterations of the book that you're holding. First and foremost is Zeke Vanderhoek, the founder of Manhattan GMAT. Zeke was a lone tutor in New York when he started the Company in 2000. Now, nine years later, MGMAT has Instructors and offices nationwide, and the Company contributes to the studies and successes of thousands of students each year.

Our 4th Edition Strategy Guides are based on the continuing experiences of our Instructors and our students. We owe much of these latest editions to the insight provided by our students. On the Company side, we are indebted to many of our Instructors, including but not limited to Josh Braslow, Dan Gonzalez, Mike Kim, Stacey Koprince, Ben Ku, Jadran Lee, David Mahler, Ron Purewal, Tate Shafer, Emily Sledge, and of course Chris Ryan, the Company's Lead Instructor and Director of Curriculum Development.

At Manhattan GMAT, we continually aspire to provide the best Instructors and resources possible. We hope that you'll find our dedication manifest in this book. If you have any comments or questions, please e-mail me at andrew.yang@manhattangmat.com. I'll be sure that your comments reach Chris and the rest of the team—and I'll read them too.

Best of luck in preparing for the GMAT!

Sincerely,

Andrew Yang
President
Manhattan GMAT

HOW TO ACCESS YOUR ONLINE RESOURCES

If you...

⊙ **are a registered Manhattan GMAT student**

and have received this book as part of your course materials, you have AUTOMATIC access to ALL of our online resources. This includes all practice exams, question banks, and online updates to this book. To access these resources, follow the instructions in the Welcome Guide provided to you at the start of your program. Do NOT follow the instructions below.

⊙ **purchased this book from the Manhattan GMAT Online store or at one of our Centers**

1. Go to: http://www.manhattangmat.com/practicecenter.cfm

2. Log in using the username and password used when your account was set up.

⊙ **purchased this book at a retail location**

1. Create an account with Manhattan GMAT at the website: https://www.manhattangmat.com/createaccount.cfm

2. Go to: http://www.manhattangmat.com/access.cfm

3. Follow the instructions on the screen.

Your one year of online access begins on the day that you register your book at the above URL.

You only need to register your product ONCE at the above URL. To use your online resources any time AFTER you have completed the registration process, login to the following URL: http://www.manhattangmat.com/practicecenter.cfm

Please note that online access is non-transferable. This means that only NEW and UNREGISTERED copies of the book will grant you online access. Previously used books will not provide any online resources.

⊙ **purchased an e-book version of this book**

1. Create an account with Manhattan GMAT at the website: https://www.manhattangmat.com/createaccount.cfm

2. Email a copy of your purchase receipt to books@manhattangmat.com to activate your resources. Please be sure to use the same email address to create an account that you used to purchase the e-book.

For any technical issues, email books@manhattangmat.com or call 800-576-4628.

Please refer to the following page for a description of the online resources that come with this book.

YOUR ONLINE RESOURCES

Your purchase includes ONLINE ACCESS to the following:

⊙ 6 Computer Adaptive Online Practice Exams

The 6 full-length computer adaptive practice exams included with the purchase of this book are delivered online using Manhattan GMAT's proprietary computer-adaptive test engine. The exams adapt to your ability level by drawing from a bank of more than 1,200 unique questions of varying difficulty levels written by Manhattan GMAT's expert instructors, all of whom have scored in the 99th percentile on the Official GMAT. At the end of each exam you will receive a score, an analysis of your results, and the opportunity to review detailed explanations for each question. You may choose to take the exams timed or untimed.

The content presented in this book is updated periodically to ensure that it reflects the GMAT's most current trends and is as accurate as possible. You may view any known errors or minor changes upon registering for online access.

Important Note: The 6 computer adaptive online exams included with the purchase of this book are the SAME exams that you receive upon purchasing ANY book in Manhattan GMAT's 8 Book Strategy Series.

⊙ *Fractions, Decimals, & Percents* Online Question Bank

The Bonus Online Question Bank for *Fractions, Decimals, & Percents* consists of 25 extra practice questions (with detailed explanations) that test the variety of concepts and skills covered in this book. These questions provide you with extra practice beyond the problem sets contained in this book. You may use our online timer to practice your pacing by setting time limits for each question in the bank.

⊙ Online Updates to the Contents in this Book

The content presented in this book is updated periodically to ensure that it reflects the GMAT's most current trends. You may view all updates, including any known errors or changes, upon registering for online access.

Part I: General

Part II: Advanced

TABLE OF CONTENTS

g

PART I: GENERAL

This part of the book covers both basic and intermediate topics within *Fractions, Decimals, & Percents*. Complete Part I before moving on to Part II: Advanced.

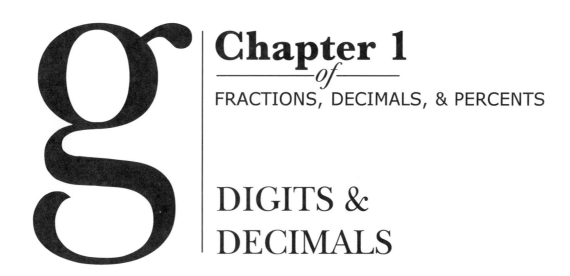

Chapter 1
of
FRACTIONS, DECIMALS, & PERCENTS

DIGITS & DECIMALS

In This Chapter . . .

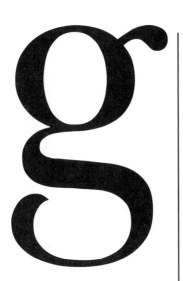

DECIMALS

GMAT math goes beyond an understanding of the properties of integers (which include the counting numbers, such as 1, 2, 3, their negative counterparts, such as −1, −2, −3, and 0). The GMAT also tests your ability to understand the numbers that fall in between the integers. Such numbers can be expressed as decimals. For example, the decimal 6.3 falls between the integers 6 and 7.

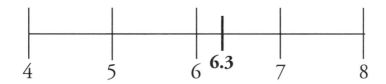

Some other examples of decimals include:

Decimals less than −1:	−3.65, −12.01, −145.9
Decimals between −1 and 0:	−0.65, −0.8912, −0.076
Decimals between 0 and 1:	0.65, 0.8912, 0.076
Decimals greater than 1:	3.65, 12.01, 145.9

Note that an integer can be expressed as a decimal by adding the decimal point and the digit 0. For example:

$$8 = 8.0 \qquad -123 = -123.0 \qquad 400 = 400.0$$

You can use a number line to decide between which whole numbers a decimal falls.

DIGITS

Every number is composed of digits. There are only ten digits in our number system: 0, 1, 2, 3, 4, 5, 6, 7, 8, 9. The term digit refers to one building block of a number; it does not refer to a number itself. For example: 356 is a number composed of three digits: 3, 5, and 6.

Integers can be classified by the number of digits they contain. For example:

2, 7, and −8 are each single-digit numbers (they are each composed of one digit).
43, 63, and −14 are each double-digit numbers (composed of two digits).
500,000 and −468,024 are each six-digit numbers (composed of six digits).
789,526,622 is a nine-digit number (composed of nine digits).

Non-integers are not generally classified by the number of digits they contain, since you can always add any number of zeroes at the end, on the right side of the decimal point:

$$9.1 = 9.10 = 9.100$$

Place Value

Every digit in a number has a particular place value depending on its location within the number. For example, in the number 452, the digit 2 is in the ones (or "units") place, the digit 5 is in the tens place, and the digit 4 is in the hundreds place. The name of each location corresponds to the "value" of that place. Thus:

2 is worth two "units" (two "ones"), or 2 (= 2 × 1).
5 is worth five tens, or 50 (= 5 × 10).
4 is worth four hundreds, or 400 (= 4 × 100).

We can now write the number 452 as the **sum** of these products:

452 = 4 × 100 + 5 × 10 + 2 × 1

You should memorize the names of all the place values.

6	9	2	5	6	7	8	9	1	0	2	3	.	8	3	4	7
HUNDRED BILLIONS	TEN BILLIONS	ONE BILLIONS	HUNDRED MILLIONS	TEN MILLIONS	ONE MILLIONS	HUNDRED THOUSANDS	TEN THOUSANDS	THOUSANDS	HUNDREDS	TENS	UNITS OR ONES		TENTHS	HUNDREDTHS	THOUSANDTHS	TEN THOUSANDTHS

The chart to the left analyzes the place value of all the digits in the number:

692,567,891,023.8347

Notice that the place values to the left of the decimal all end in "-s," while the place values to the right of the decimal all end in "-ths." This is because the suffix "-ths" gives these places (to the right of the decimal) a fractional value.

Let us analyze the end of the preceding number: **0.8347**

8 is in the tenths place, giving it a value of 8 tenths, or $\dfrac{8}{10}$.

3 is in the hundredths place, giving it a value of 3 hundredths, or $\dfrac{3}{100}$.

4 is in the thousandths place, giving it a value of 4 thousandths, or $\dfrac{4}{1000}$.

7 is in the ten thousandths place, giving it a value of 7 ten thousandths, or $\dfrac{7}{10,000}$.

To use a concrete example, 0.8 might mean eight tenths of one dollar, which would be 8 dimes or 80 cents. Additionally, 0.03 might mean three hundredths of one dollar, which would be 3 pennies or 3 cents.

Using Place Value on the GMAT

Some difficult GMAT problems require the use of place value with unknown digits.

> *A* and *B* are both two–digit numbers, with *A* > *B*. If *A* and *B* contain the same digits, but in reverse order, what integer must be a factor of (*A* − *B*)?
>
> (A) 4   (B) 5   (C) 6   (D) 8   (E) 9

To solve this problem, assign two variables to be the digits in *A* and *B*: *x* and *y*.
Let $A = \boxed{x}\boxed{y}$ (**not** the product of *x* and *y*: *x* is in the tens place, and *y* is in the units place). The boxes remind you that *x* and *y* stand for digits. *A* is therefore the sum of *x* tens and *y* ones. Using algebra, we write $A = 10x + y$.

Since *B*'s digits are reversed, $B = \boxed{y}\boxed{x}$. Algebraically, *B* can be expressed as $10y + x$. The difference of *A* and *B* can be expressed as follows:

$$A - B = 10x + y - (10y + x) = 9x - 9y = 9(x - y)$$

Clearly, 9 must be a factor of $A - B$. The correct answer is **(E)**.

You can also make up digits for *x* and *y* and plug them in to create *A* and *B*. This will not necessarily yield the unique right answer, but it should help you eliminate wrong choices.

In general, for unknown digits problems, be ready to create variables (such as *x*, *y*, and *z*) to represent the unknown digits. Recognize that each unknown is restricted to at most 10 possible values (0 through 9). Then apply any given constraints, which may involve number properties such as divisibility or odds & evens.

Place value can help you solve tough problems about digits.

Rounding to the Nearest Place Value

The GMAT occasionally requires you to round a number to a specific place value.

> What is 3.681 rounded to the nearest tenth?

First, find the digit located in the specified place value. The digit 6 is in the tenths place.

Second, look at the right-digit-neighbor (the digit immediately to the right) of the digit in question. In this case, 8 is the right-digit-neighbor of 6. If the right-digit-neighbor is 5 or greater, round the digit in question UP. Otherwise, leave the digit alone. In this case, since 8 is greater than five, the digit in question (6) must be rounded up to 7. Thus, 3.681 rounded to the nearest tenth equals 3.7. Note that all the digits to the right of the right-digit-neighbor are irrelevant when rounding.

Rounding appears on the GMAT in the form of questions such as this:

> If *x* is the decimal 8.1*d*5, with *d* as an unknown digit, and *x* rounded to the nearest tenth is equal to 8.1, which digits could not be the value of *d*?

In order for *x* to be 8.1 when rounded to the nearest tenth, the right-digit-neighbor, *d*, must be less than 5. Therefore *d* cannot be 5, 6, 7, 8 or 9.

*Manhattan***GMAT** Prep

Adding Zeroes to Decimals

Adding zeroes to the end of a decimal or taking zeroes away from the end of a decimal does not change the value of the decimal. For example: $3.6 = 3.60 = 3.6000$

Be careful, however, not to add or remove any zeroes from within a number. Doing so will change the value of the number: $7.01 \neq 7.1$

Powers of 10: Shifting the Decimal

Place values continually decrease from left to right by powers of 10. Understanding this can help you understand the following shortcuts for multiplication and division.

When you multiply any number by a positive power of ten, move the decimal forward (right) the specified number of places. This makes positive numbers larger:

> When you shift the decimal to the right, the number gets bigger. When you shift the decimal to the left, the number gets smaller.

In words	thousands	hundreds	tens	ones	tenths	hundredths	thousandths
In numbers	1000	100	10	1	0.1	0.01	0.001
In powers of ten	10^3	10^2	10^1	10^0	10^{-1}	10^{-2}	10^{-3}

$3.9742 \times 10^3 = 3{,}974.2$ (Move the decimal forward 3 spaces.)
$89.507 \times 10 = 895.07$ (Move the decimal forward 1 space.)

When you divide any number by a positive power of ten, move the decimal backward (left) the specified number of places. This makes positive numbers smaller:

$4{,}169.2 \div 10^2 = 41.692$ (Move the decimal backward 2 spaces.)
$89.507 \div 10 = 8.9507$ (Move the decimal backward 1 space.)

Note that if you need to add zeroes in order to shift a decimal, you should do so:

$2.57 \times 10^6 = 2{,}570{,}000$ (Add 4 zeroes at the end.)
$14.29 \div 10^5 = 0.0001429$ (Add 3 zeroes at the beginning.)

Finally, note that negative powers of ten reverse the regular process:

$6{,}782.01 \times 10^{-3} = 6.78201$ $53.0447 \div 10^{-2} = 5{,}304.47$

You can think about these processes as **trading decimal places for powers of ten**.

For instance, all of the following numbers equal 110,700.

110.7	$\times$	10^3
11.07	$\times$	10^4
1.107	$\times$	10^5
0.1107	$\times$	10^6
0.01107	$\times$	10^7

The first number gets smaller by a factor of 10 as we move the decimal one place to the left, but the second number gets bigger by a factor of 10 to compensate.

The Last Digit Shortcut

Sometimes the GMAT asks you to find a units digit, or a remainder after division by 10.

> What is the units digit of $(7)^2(9)^2(3)^3$?

In this problem, you can use the Last Digit Shortcut:

> To find the units digit of a product or a sum of integers, only pay attention to the units digits of the numbers you are working with. Drop any other digits.

This shortcut works because only units digits contribute to the units digit of the product.

STEP 1: $7 \times 7 = 49$ Drop the tens digit and keep only the last digit: 9.
STEP 2: $9 \times 9 = 81$ Drop the tens digit and keep only the last digit: 1.
STEP 3: $3 \times 3 \times 3 = 27$ Drop the tens digit and keep only the last digit: 7.
STEP 4: $9 \times 1 \times 7 = 63$ Multiply the last digits of each of the products.

The units digit of the final product is 3.

The Heavy Division Shortcut

Some division problems involving decimals can look rather complex. But sometimes, you only need to find an approximate solution. In these cases, you often can save yourself time by using the Heavy Division Shortcut: move the decimals in the same direction and round to whole numbers.

> What is $1{,}530{,}794 \div (31.49 \times 10^4)$ to the nearest whole number?

Step 1: Set up the division problem in fraction form: $\dfrac{1{,}530{,}794}{31.49 \times 10^4}$

Step 2: Rewrite the problem, eliminating powers of 10: $\dfrac{1{,}530{,}794}{314{,}900}$

Step 3: Your goal is to get a single digit to the left of the decimal in the denominator. In this problem, you need to move the decimal point backward 5 spaces. You can do this to the denominator as long as you do the same thing to the numerator. (Technically, what you are doing is dividing top and bottom by the same power of 10: 100,000)

$$\frac{1{,}530{,}794}{314{,}900} = \frac{15.30794}{3.14900}$$

Now you have the single digit 3 to the left of the decimal in the denominator.

Step 4: Focus only on the whole number parts of the numerator and denominator and solve. $\dfrac{15.30794}{3.14900} \cong \dfrac{15}{3} = 5$

An approximate answer to this complex division problem is 5. If this answer is not precise enough, keep one more decimal place and do long division (eg., $153 \div 31 \approx 4.9$).

Use the Heavy Division Shortcut when you need an approximate answer.

Decimal Operations

ADDITION AND SUBTRACTION

To add or subtract decimals, make sure to line up the decimal points. Then add zeroes to make the right sides of the decimals the same length.

4.319 + 221.8		**10 − 0.063**	
Line up the decimal points and add zeroes.	4.319 + 221.800 226.119	Line up the decimal points and add zeroes.	10.000 − 0.063 9.937

Addition & Subtraction: Line up the decimal points!

MULTIPLICATION

To multiply decimals, ignore the decimal point until the end. Just multiply the numbers as you would if they were whole numbers. Then count the *total* number of digits to the right of the decimal point in the factors. The product should have the same number of digits to the right of the decimal point.

0.02 × 1.4   Multiply normally: 14
                                            × 2
                                            28

There are 3 digits to the right of the decimal point in the factors (0 and 2 in the first factor and 4 in the second factor). Therefore, move the decimal point 3 places to the left in the product: 28 → 0.028.

Multiplication: In the factors, count all the digits to the right of the decimal point— then put that many digits to the right of the decimal point in the product.

If the product ends with 0, count it in this process: 0.8 × 0.5 = 0.40, since 8 × 5 = 40.

If you are multiplying a very large number and a very small number, the following trick works to simplify the calculation: move the decimals **in the opposite direction** the same number of places.

0.0003 × 40,000 = ?

Move the decimal point RIGHT four places on the 0.0003 → 3
Move the decimal point LEFT four places on the 40,000 → 4

0.0003 × 40,000 = 3 × 4 = 12

The reason this technique works is that you are multiplying and then dividing by the same power of ten. In other words, you are **trading decimal places** in one number for decimal places in another number. This is just like trading decimal places for powers of ten, as we saw earlier.

DIVISION

If there is a decimal point in the dividend (the inner number) only, you can simply bring the decimal point straight up to the answer and divide normally.

Ex. **12.42 ÷ 3** = 4.14

$$\begin{array}{r} 4.14 \\ 3\overline{)12.42} \\ \underline{12} \\ 04 \\ \underline{3} \\ 12 \end{array}$$

However, if there is a decimal point in the divisor (the outer number), you should shift the decimal point in both the divisor and the dividend to make the *divisor* a whole number. Then, bring the decimal point up and divide.

Ex: **12.42÷ 0.3** → 124.2 ÷ 3 = 41.4

$$\begin{array}{r} 41.4 \\ 3\overline{)124.2} \\ \underline{12} \\ 04 \\ \underline{3} \\ 12 \end{array}$$

Move the decimal one space to the right to make 0.3 a whole number. Then, move the decimal one space in 12.42 to make it 124.2.

Division: Divide by whole numbers!

You can always simplify division problems that involve decimals by shifting the decimal point **in the same direction** in both the divisor and the dividend, even when the division problem is expressed as a fraction:

$$\frac{0.0045}{0.09} = \frac{45}{900}$$

Move the decimal 4 spaces to the right to make both the numerator and the denominator whole numbers.

Note that this is essentially the same process as simplifying a fraction. You are simply multiplying the numerator and denominator of the fraction by a power of ten—in this case, 10^4, or 10,000.

Keep track of how you move the decimal point! To simplify multiplication, you can move decimals in opposite directions. But to simplify division, you move decimals in the same direction.

Equivalently, by adding zeroes, you can express the numerator and the denominator as the same units, then simplify:

$$\frac{0.0045}{0.09} = \frac{0.0045}{0.0900} = 45 \text{ ten thousandths} \div 900 \text{ ten–thousandths} = \frac{45}{900} = \frac{5}{100} = 0.05$$

Remember, in order to divide decimals, you must make the OUTER number a whole number by shifting the decimal point.

*Manhattan*GMAT*Prep
the new standard

POWERS AND ROOTS

To square or cube a decimal, you can always simply multiply it by itself once or twice. However, to raise a decimal to a larger power, you can rewrite the decimal as the product of an integer and a power of ten, and then apply the exponent.

$$(0.5)^4 = ?$$

Rewrite the decimal:　　　　　　　　　$0.5 = 5 \times 10^{-1}$

Apply the exponent to each part:　　　$(5 \times 10^{-1})^4 = 5^4 \times 10^{-4}$

Compute the first part and combine:　$5^4 = 25^2 = 625$
　　　　　　　　　　　　　　　　　　$625 \times 10^{-4} = 0.0625$

Take a power or a root of a decimal by splitting the decimal into 2 parts: an integer and a power of ten.

Solve for roots of decimals the same way. Recall that a root is a number raised to a fractional power: a square root is a number raised to the 1/2 power, a cube root is a number raised to the 1/3 power, etc.

$$\sqrt[3]{0.000027} = ?$$

Rewrite the decimal. Make the first number something you can take the cube root of easily:
$$0.000027 = 27 \times 10^{-6}$$

Write the root as a fractional exponent:　　$(0.000027)^{1/3} = (27 \times 10^{-6})^{1/3}$

Apply the exponent to each part:　　　　　$(27)^{1/3} \times (10^{-6})^{1/3} = (27)^{1/3} \times 10^{-2}$

Compute the first part and combine:　　　$(27)^{1/3} = 3$　　(since $3^3 = 27$)
　　　　　　　　　　　　　　　　　　　　$3 \times 10^{-2} = 0.03$

Powers and roots: Rewrite the decimal using powers of ten!

Once you understand the principles, you can take a shortcut by counting decimal places. For instance, the number of decimal places in the result of a cubed decimal is 3 times the number of decimal places in the original decimal:

$$(0.04)^3 = 0.000064 \qquad \underset{2 \; places}{(0.04)^3} \qquad \underset{2 \times 3 = 6 \; places}{= 0.000064}$$

Likewise, the number of decimal places in a cube root is 1/3 the number of decimal places in the original decimal:

$$\sqrt[3]{0.000000008} = 0.002 \qquad \underset{9 \; places}{\sqrt[3]{0.000000008}} \qquad \underset{9 \div 3 = 3 \; places}{= 0.002}$$

However, make sure that you can work with powers of ten using exponent rules.

*Manhattan*GMAT*Prep
the new standard

Problem Set

Solve each problem, applying the concepts and rules you learned in this section.

1. What is the units digit of $(2)^5(3)^3(4)^2$?

2. What is the sum of all the possible 3-digit numbers that can be constructed using the digits 3, 4, and 5, if each digit can be used only once in each number?

3. In the decimal, 2.4d7, d represents a digit from 0 to 9. If the value of the decimal rounded to the nearest tenth is less than 2.5, what are the possible values of d?

4. If k is an integer, and if 0.02468×10^k is greater than 10,000, what is the least possible value of k?

5. Which integer values of b would give the number $2002 \div 10^{-b}$ a value between 1 and 100?

6. Estimate to the nearest 10,000: $\dfrac{4{,}509{,}982{,}344}{5.342 \times 10^4}$

7. Simplify: $(4.5 \times 2 + 6.6) \div 0.003$

8. Simplify: $(4 \times 10^{-2}) - (2.5 \times 10^{-3})$

9. What is $4{,}563{,}021 \div 10^5$, rounded to the nearest whole number?

10. Simplify: $(0.08)^2 \div 0.4$

11. Data Sufficiency: The number A is a two-digit positive integer; the number B is the two-digit positive integer formed by reversing the digits of A. If $Q = 10B - A$, what is the value of Q?

    (1) The tens digit of A is 7.
    (2) The tens digit of B is 6.

12. Simplify: $[8 - (1.08 + 6.9)]^2$

13. Which integer values of j would give the number $-37{,}129 \times 10^j$ a value between -100 and -1?

14.   Simplify: $\dfrac{0.00081}{0.09}$

15.   Simplify: $\sqrt[8]{0.00000256}$

1. **4:** Use the Last Digit Shortcut, ignoring all digits but the last in any intermediate products:

    STEP ONE: $2^5 = 32$ Drop the tens digit and keep only the last digit: 2.

    STEP TWO: $3^3 = 27$ Drop the tens digit and keep only the last digit: 7.

    STEP THREE: $4^2 = 16$ Drop the tens digit and keep only the last digit: 6.

    STEP FOUR: $2 \times 7 \times 6 = 84$ Drop the tens digit and keep only the last digit: 4.

2. **2664:** There are 6 ways in which to arrange these digits: 345, 354, 435, 453, 534, and 543. Notice that each digit appears twice in the hundreds column, twice in the tens column, and twice in the ones column. Therefore, you can use your knowledge of place value to find the sum quickly:

$$100(24) + 10(24) + (24) = 2400 + 240 + 24 = 2664.$$

3. **{0, 1, 2, 3, 4}:** If d is 5 or greater, the decimal rounded to the nearest tenth will be 2.5.

4. **6:** Multiplying 0.02468 by a positive power of ten will shift the decimal point to the right. Simply shift the decimal point to the right until the result is greater than 10,000. Keep track of how many times you shift the decimal point. Shifting the decimal point 5 times results in 2,468. This is still less than 10,000. Shifting one more place yields 24,680, which is greater than 10,000.

5. **{−2, −3}:** In order to give 2002 a value between 1 and 100, we must shift the decimal point to change the number to 2.002 or 20.02. This requires a shift of either two or three places to the left. Remember that, while multiplication shifts the decimal point to the right, division shifts it to the left. To shift the decimal point 2 places to the left, we would divide by 10^2. To shift it 3 places to the left, we would divide by 10^3. Therefore, the exponent $-b = \{2, 3\}$, and $b = \{-2, -3\}$.

6. **90,000:** Use the Heavy Division Shortcut to estimate:

$$\frac{4,509,982,344}{53,420} \approx \frac{4,500,000,000}{50,000} = \frac{450,000}{5} = 90,000$$

7. **5,200:** Use the order of operations, PEMDAS (Parentheses, Exponents, Multiplication & Division, Addition and Subtraction) to simplify.

$$\frac{9 + 6.6}{0.003} = \frac{15.6}{0.003} = \frac{15,600}{3} = 5,200$$

8. **0.0375:** First, rewrite the numbers in standard notation by shifting the decimal point. Then, add zeroes, line up the decimal points, and subtract.

$$\begin{array}{r} 0.0400 \\ - \ 0.0025 \\ \hline 0.0375 \end{array}$$

9. **46:** To divide by a positive power of 10, shift the decimal point to the left. This yields 45.63021. To round to the nearest whole number, look at the tenths place. The digit in the tenths place, 6, is more than five. Therefore, the number is closest to 46.

10. **0.016:** Use the order of operations, PEMDAS (Parentheses, Exponents, Multiplication & Division, Addition and Subtraction) to simplify. Shift the decimals in the numerator and denominator so that you are dividing by an integer.

$$\frac{(0.08)^2}{0.4} = \frac{0.0064}{0.4} = \frac{0.064}{4} = 0.016$$

*Manhattan*GMAT*Prep

11. **(B) Statement (2) ALONE is sufficient, but statement (1) alone is not sufficient.** Write A as XY, where X and Y are digits (X is the tens digit of A and Y is the units digit of A). Then B can be written as YX, with reversed digits. Writing these numbers in algebraic rather than digital form, we have $A = 10X + Y$ and $B = 10Y + X$. Therefore, $Q = 10B - A = 10(10Y + X) - (10X + Y) = 100Y + 10X - 10X - Y = 99Y$. The value of Q only depends on the value of Y, which is the tens digit of B. The value of X is irrelevant to Q. Therefore, statement (2) alone is SUFFICIENT.

You can also make up and test numbers to get the same result, but algebra is faster and more transparent. For instance, if we take $Y = 7$, then $Q = 693$, which contains no 7's digits. Thus, it may be hard to see how Q depends on Y.

12. **0.0004:** Use the order of operations, PEMDAS (Parentheses, Exponents, Multiplication & Division, Addition and Subtraction) to simplify.

First, add $1.08 + 6.9$ by lining up the decimal points:

$$
\begin{array}{r}
1.08 \\
+\,6.9 \\
\hline
7.98
\end{array}
$$

Then, subtract 7.98 from 8 by lining up the decimal points, adding zeroes to make the decimals the same length:

$$
\begin{array}{r}
8.00 \\
-7.98 \\
\hline
0.02
\end{array}
$$

Finally, square 0.02, conserving the number of digits to the right of the decimal point.

$$
\begin{array}{r}
0.02 \\
\times\,0.02 \\
\hline
0.0004
\end{array}
$$

13. **{−3, −4}:** In order to give −37,129 a value between −100 and −1, we must shift the decimal point to change the number to −37.129 or −3.7129. This requires a shift of either two or three places to the left. Remember that multiplication shifts the decimal point to the right. To shift the decimal point 3 places to the left, we would multiply by 10^{-3}. To shift it 4 places to the left, we would multiply by 10^{-4}. Therefore, the exponent $j = \{-3, -4\}$.

14. **0.009:** Shift the decimal point 2 spaces to eliminate the decimal point in the denominator.

$$\frac{0.00081}{0.09} = \frac{0.081}{9}$$

Then divide. First, drop the 3 decimal places: $81 \div 9 = 9$. Then put the 3 decimal places back: 0.009

15. **0.2:** Write the expression as a decimal raised to a fractional power, using powers of ten to separate the base from the exponent: $(0.00000256)^{1/8} = (256)^{1/8} \times (10^{-8})^{1/8}$. Now, you can compute each component separately and combine them at the finish: $(256)^{1/8} \times (10^{-8})^{1/8} = 2 \times 10^{-1} = 0.2$.

Chapter 2
of
FRACTIONS, DECIMALS, & PERCENTS

FRACTIONS

In This Chapter . . .

FRACTIONS

Decimals are one way of expressing the numbers that fall in between the integers. Another way of expressing these numbers is fractions.

For example, the fraction $\frac{13}{2}$, which equals 6.5, falls between the integers 6 and 7.

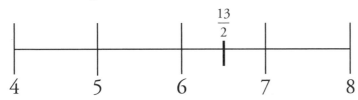

Proper fractions are those that fall between 0 and 1. In proper fractions, the numerator is always smaller than the denominator. For example:

$$\frac{1}{4}, \frac{1}{2}, \frac{2}{3}, \frac{7}{10}$$

Improper fractions are those that are greater than 1. In improper fractions, the numerator is greater than the denominator. For example:

$$\frac{5}{4}, \frac{13}{2}, \frac{11}{3}, \frac{101}{10}$$

Improper fractions can be rewritten as **mixed numbers**. A mixed number is an integer and a proper fraction. For example:

$$\frac{5}{4} = 1\frac{1}{4} \qquad\qquad \frac{13}{2} = 6\frac{1}{2} \qquad\qquad \frac{11}{3} = 3\frac{2}{3} \qquad\qquad \frac{101}{10} = 10\frac{1}{10}$$

Although all the preceding examples use positive fractions, note that fractions and mixed numbers can be negative as well.

Proper and improper fractions behave differently in many cases.

Numerator and Denominator Rules

Certain key rules govern the relationship between the numerator (the top number) and the denominator (the bottom number) of proper fractions. These rules are important to internalize, but keep in mind that, as written, they **only apply to positive fractions.**

As the NUMERATOR goes up, the fraction INCREASES. If you increase the numerator of a fraction, while holding the denominator constant, the fraction increases in value.

$$\frac{1}{8} < \frac{2}{8} < \frac{3}{8} < \frac{4}{8} < \frac{5}{8} < \frac{6}{8} < \frac{7}{8} < \frac{8}{8} < \frac{9}{8} < \frac{10}{8} < ...$$

As the DENOMINATOR goes up, the fraction DECREASES. If you increase the denominator of a fraction, while holding the numerator constant, the fraction decreases in value as it approaches 0.

$$\frac{3}{2} > \frac{3}{3} > \frac{3}{4} > \frac{3}{5} > \frac{3}{6} ... > \frac{3}{1000} ... \rightarrow 0$$

Adding the same number to BOTH the numerator and the denominator brings the fraction CLOSER TO 1, regardless of the fraction's value.

If the fraction is originally smaller than 1, the fraction **increases** in value as it approaches 1.

$$\frac{1}{2} < \frac{1+1}{2+1} = \frac{2}{3} < \frac{2+9}{3+9} = \frac{11}{12} < \frac{11+1000}{12+1000} = \frac{1011}{1012}$$

Thus: $\qquad \frac{1}{2} < \frac{2}{3} < \frac{11}{12} < \frac{1011}{1012} ... \rightarrow 1$

Conversely, if the fraction is originally larger than 1, the fraction **decreases** in value as it approaches 1.

$$\frac{3}{2} > \frac{3+1}{2+1} = \frac{4}{3} > \frac{4+9}{3+9} = \frac{13}{12} > \frac{13+1000}{12+1000} = \frac{1013}{1012}$$

Thus: $\qquad \frac{3}{2} > \frac{4}{3} > \frac{13}{12} > \frac{1013}{1012} ... \rightarrow 1$

*Manhattan*GMAT*Prep
the new standard

These rules only apply to positive proper fractions!

Simplifying Fractions

Simplifying fractions is a process that attempts to express a fraction in its lowest terms. Fractional answers on the GMAT will always be presented in fully simplified form. The process of simplifying is governed by one simple rule:

MULTIPLYING or DIVIDING both the numerator and the denominator by the same number does not change the value of the fraction.

$$\frac{4}{5} = \frac{4(3)}{5(3)} = \frac{12}{15} = \frac{12(2)}{15(2)} = \frac{24}{30} \qquad \frac{24}{30} = \frac{24 \div 6}{30 \div 6} = \frac{4}{5}$$

Simplifying a fraction means dividing both the numerator and the denominator by a common factor. This must be repeated until no common factors remain.

$$\frac{40}{30} = \frac{40 \div 5}{30 \div 5} = \frac{8}{6} = \frac{8 \div 2}{6 \div 2} = \frac{4}{3} \quad \text{or in one step:} \quad \frac{40}{30} = \frac{40 \div 10}{30 \div 10} = \frac{4}{3}$$

Simplify fractions by multiplying or dividing both the numerator and the denominator by the same number.

Converting Improper Fractions to Mixed Numbers

To convert an improper fraction into a mixed number, simply divide the numerator by the denominator, stopping when you reach a remainder smaller than the denominator.

$$\frac{9}{4} = 9 \div 4 = 4\overline{)9} \\ \underline{8} \\ 1$$

Since $9 \div 4 = 2$ with a remainder of 1, we can write the improper fraction as the integer 2 with a fractional part of 1 over the original denominator of 4.

Thus, $\frac{9}{4} = 2\frac{1}{4}$.

This process can also work in reverse. In order to convert a mixed number into an improper fraction (something you need to do in order to multiply or divide mixed numbers), use the following procedure:

$2\frac{1}{4}$ Multiply the whole number (2) by the denominator (4) and add the numerator (1):

$2 \times 4 + 1 = 9$ Now place the number 9 over the original denominator, 4: $\frac{9}{4}$

Alternatively, since $2\frac{1}{4} = 2 + \frac{1}{4}$, just split the mixed fraction into its two parts and rewrite the whole number using a common denominator:

$$2\frac{1}{4} = 2 + \frac{1}{4} = \frac{8}{4} + \frac{1}{4} = \frac{9}{4}$$

*Manhattan*GMAT*Prep
the new standard

The Multiplication Shortcut

To multiply fractions, first multiply the numerators together, then multiply the denominators together, and finally simplify your resulting product by expressing it in lowest terms. For example:

$$\frac{8}{15} \times \frac{35}{72} = \frac{8(35)}{15(72)} = \frac{280}{1080} = \frac{28}{108} = \frac{7}{27}$$

There is, however, a shortcut that can make fraction multiplication much less tedious. The shortcut is to simplify your products BEFORE multiplying. This is also known as "cancelling."

Notice that the **8** in the numerator and the **72** in the denominator both have 8 as a factor. Thus, they can be simplified from $\frac{8}{72}$ to $\frac{1}{9}$.

Notice also that **35** in the numerator and **15** in the denominator both have 5 as a factor. Thus, they can be simplified from $\frac{35}{15}$ to $\frac{7}{3}$.

Now the multiplication will be easier and no further simplification will be necessary:

$$\frac{8}{15} \times \frac{35}{72} = \frac{8(35)}{15(72)} = \frac{1(7)}{3(9)} = \frac{7}{27}$$

Always try to cancel factors before multiplying fractions!

In order to multiply mixed numbers, you should first convert each mixed number into an improper fraction:

$$2\frac{1}{3} \times 6\frac{3}{5} = \frac{7}{3} \times \frac{33}{5}$$

You can simplify the problem, using the multiplication shortcut of cancelling, and then convert the result to a mixed number:

$$\frac{7}{3} \times \frac{33}{5} = \frac{7(33)}{3(5)} = \frac{7(11)}{1(5)} = \frac{77}{5} = 15\frac{2}{5}$$

This shortcut is known as "cancelling."

No Addition or Subtraction Shortcuts

While shortcuts are very useful when multiplying fractions, you must be careful NOT to take any shortcuts when adding or subtracting fractions. In order to add or subtract fractions, you must:

> (1) find a common denominator
> (2) change each fraction so that it is expressed using this common denominator
> (3) add up the numerators only

You may need to simplify the result when you are finished; the resulting fraction may not be in reduced form.

<table>
<tr>
<td>

$$\frac{3}{8} + \frac{7}{12}$$

</td>
<td>

A common denominator is 24. Thus, $\frac{3}{8} = \frac{9}{24}$ and $\frac{7}{12} = \frac{14}{24}$.

</td>
</tr>
<tr>
<td>

$$\frac{9}{24} + \frac{14}{24}$$

</td>
<td>

Express each fraction using the common denominator 24.

</td>
</tr>
<tr>
<td>

$$\frac{9}{24} + \frac{14}{24} = \frac{23}{24}$$

</td>
<td>

Finally, add the numerators to find the answer.

</td>
</tr>
</table>

To add and subtract fractions, you must find a common denominator.

Another example:

<table>
<tr>
<td>

$$\frac{11}{15} - \frac{7}{30}$$

</td>
<td>

A common denominator is 30. $\frac{11}{15} = \frac{22}{30}$ and $\frac{7}{30}$ stays the same.

</td>
</tr>
<tr>
<td>

$$\frac{22}{30} - \frac{7}{30}$$

</td>
<td>

Express each fraction using the common denominator 30.

</td>
</tr>
<tr>
<td>

$$\frac{22}{30} - \frac{7}{30} = \frac{15}{30}$$

</td>
<td>

Subtract the numerators.

</td>
</tr>
<tr>
<td>

$$\frac{15}{30} = \frac{1}{2}$$

</td>
<td>

Simplify $\frac{15}{30}$ to find the answer: $\frac{1}{2}$.

</td>
</tr>
</table>

In order to add or subtract mixed numbers, you can convert to improper fractions, or you can set up the problem vertically and solve the fraction first and the whole number last.

Addition	**Subtraction**
$7\frac{1}{3} = 7\frac{2}{6}$	$7\frac{1}{3} = 7\frac{2}{6} = 7 + \frac{2}{6}$
$+\ 4\frac{1}{2} = 4\frac{3}{6}$	$-\ 4\frac{1}{2} = 4\frac{3}{6} = 4 + \frac{3}{6}$
$11\frac{5}{6}$	$3 + \frac{-1}{6} = 2 + \frac{5}{6} = 2\frac{5}{6}$

You may wind up with a negative fraction. Simply combine it afterwards with the whole number as shown below.

Dividing Fractions: Use the Reciprocal

In order to divide fractions, you must first understand the concept of the reciprocal. You can think of the reciprocal as the fraction flipped upside down.

The reciprocal of $\frac{3}{4}$ is $\frac{4}{3}$.   The reciprocal of $\frac{2}{9}$ is $\frac{9}{2}$.

What is the reciprocal of an integer? Think of an integer as a fraction with a denominator of 1. Thus, the integer 5 is really just $\frac{5}{1}$. To find the reciprocal, just flip it.

The reciprocal of **5** or $\frac{5}{1}$ is $\frac{1}{5}$.   The reciprocal of **8** is $\frac{1}{8}$.

To check if you have found the reciprocal of a number, use this rule: **The product of a number and its reciprocal always equals 1.** The following examples reveal this to be true:

$$\frac{3}{4} \times \frac{4}{3} = \frac{12}{12} = 1 \qquad 5 \times \frac{1}{5} = \frac{5}{1} \times \frac{1}{5} = \frac{5}{5} = 1 \qquad \sqrt{7} \times \frac{\sqrt{7}}{7} = \frac{\sqrt{7}}{1} \times \frac{\sqrt{7}}{7} = \frac{7}{7} = 1$$

In order to divide fractions,

    (1) change the divisor into its reciprocal, and then

    (2) multiply the fractions. Note that the divisor is the second number:

$\frac{1}{2} \div \frac{3}{4}$ First, change the divisor $\frac{3}{4}$ into its reciprocal $\frac{4}{3}$.

$\frac{1}{2} \times \frac{4}{3} = \frac{4}{6} = \frac{2}{3}$ Then, multiply the fractions and simplify to lowest terms.

In order to divide mixed numbers, first change them into improper fractions:

$5\frac{2}{3} \div 8\frac{1}{2} = \frac{17}{3} \div \frac{17}{2}$ Then, change the divisor $\frac{17}{2}$ into its reciprocal $\frac{2}{17}$.

$\frac{17}{3} \times \frac{2}{17} = \frac{2}{3}$ Multiply the fractions, cancelling where you can.

To divide fractions, flip the second fraction and multiply.

Division in Disguise

Sometimes, dividing fractions can be written in a confusing way. Consider one of the previous examples:

$\dfrac{1}{2} \div \dfrac{3}{4}$ can also be written as a "double–decker" fraction this way: $\dfrac{\dfrac{1}{2}}{\dfrac{3}{4}}$

Do not be confused. You can rewrite this as the top fraction divided by the bottom fraction, and solve it normally (by using the reciprocal of the bottom fraction and then multiplying).

$$\frac{\frac{1}{2}}{\frac{3}{4}} = \frac{1}{2} \div \frac{3}{4} = \frac{1}{2} \times \frac{4}{3} = \frac{4}{6} = \frac{2}{3}$$

Also notice that you can often simplify quickly by multiplying both top and bottom by a common denominator:

$$\frac{\frac{1}{2}}{\frac{3}{4}} = \frac{\frac{1}{2} \times 4}{\frac{3}{4} \times 4} = \frac{2}{3}$$

Multiplying and dividing positive proper fractions may yield unexpected results.

Fraction Operations: Funky Results

Adding and subtracting fractions leads to expected results. When you add two positive fractions, you get a larger number. When you subtract a positive fraction from something else, you get a smaller number.

However, multiplication and division of proper fractions (fractions between 0 and 1) yields UNEXPECTED results. Multiplying two proper fractions yields a SMALLER number. Dividing two proper fractions yields a LARGER number.

OPERATION EXAMPLE		INCREASE OR DECREASE
Adding Fractions	$\dfrac{3}{5} + \dfrac{1}{5} = \dfrac{4}{5}$	**INCREASE:** Similar to adding positive integers, adding fractions increases their value.
Subtracting Fractions	$\dfrac{3}{5} - \dfrac{1}{5} = \dfrac{2}{5}$	**DECREASE:** Similar to subtracting positive integers, subtracting fractions decreases their value.
Multiplying Fractions	$\dfrac{3}{5} \times \dfrac{1}{5} = \dfrac{3}{25}$	**DECREASE:** Unlike multiplying positive integers, multiplying fractions decreases their value.
Dividing Fractions	$\dfrac{3}{5} \div \dfrac{1}{5} = \dfrac{3}{5} \times \dfrac{5}{1} = 3$	**INCREASE:** Unlike dividing positive integers, dividing fractions increases their value.

Comparing Fractions: Cross–Multiply

Which fraction is greater, $\frac{7}{9}$ or $\frac{4}{5}$?

The traditional method of comparing fractions involves finding a common denominator and comparing the two fractions. The common denominator of 9 and 5 is 45.

Thus, $\frac{7}{9} = \frac{35}{45}$ and $\frac{4}{5} = \frac{36}{45}$. We can see that $\frac{4}{5}$ is slightly bigger than $\frac{7}{9}$.

However, there is a shortcut to comparing fractions called cross–multiplication. This is a process that involves multiplying the numerator of one fraction with the denominator of the other fraction, and vice versa:

$$\frac{7}{9} \bowtie \frac{4}{5}$$ Set up the fractions next to each other.

(7×5) (4×9) Cross–multiply the fractions and put each answer by the
    35   36   corresponding <u>numerator</u> (NOT the denominator!)

$\frac{7}{9}$ $<$ $\frac{4}{5}$ Since 35 is less than 36, the first fraction must be less than the
second one.

This process can save you a lot of time when comparing fractions (usually more than two!) on the GMAT.

Never Split the Denominator

One final rule, perhaps the most important one, is one that you must always remember when working with complex fractions. A complex fraction is a fraction in which there is a sum or a difference in the numerator or the denominator. Three examples of complex fractions are:

(a) $\dfrac{15 + 10}{5}$ (b) $\dfrac{5}{15 + 10}$ (c) $\dfrac{15 + 10}{5 + 2}$

In example (a), the numerator is expressed as a sum.
In example (b), the denominator is expressed as a sum.
In example (c), both the numerator and the denominator are expressed as sums.

When simplifying fractions that incorporate sums or differences, remember this rule: You may split up the terms of the numerator, but you may NEVER split the terms of the DENOMINATOR.

Thus, the terms in example (a) may be split:

$$\frac{15 + 10}{5} = \frac{15}{5} + \frac{10}{5} = 3 + 2 = 5$$

But the terms in example (b) may not be split:

$$\frac{5}{15+10} \neq \frac{5}{15} + \frac{5}{10} \text{ NO!}$$

Instead, simplify the denominator first:

$$\frac{5}{15 + 10} = \frac{5}{25} = \frac{1}{5}$$

The terms in example (c) may not be split either:

$$\frac{15 + 10}{5 + 2} \neq \frac{15}{5} + \frac{10}{2} \text{ NO!}$$

Instead, simplify both parts of the fraction:

$$\frac{15 + 10}{5 + 2} = \frac{25}{7} = 3\frac{4}{7}$$

Often, GMAT problems will involve complex fractions with variables. On these problems, it is tempting to split the denominator. Do not fall for it!

It is tempting to perform the following simplification:

$$\frac{5x - 2y}{x - y} = \frac{5x}{x} - \frac{2y}{y} = 5 - 2 = 3$$

But this is **WRONG** because you cannot split terms in the denominator.

The reality is that $\frac{5x - 2y}{x - y}$ cannot be simplified further.

On the other hand, the expression $\frac{6x - 15y}{10}$ can be simplified by splitting the

difference, because this difference appears in the numerator.

$$\text{Thus: } \frac{6x - 15y}{10} = \frac{6x}{10} - \frac{15y}{10} = \frac{3x}{5} - \frac{3y}{2}$$

Benchmark Values

You will use a variety of estimating strategies on the GMAT. One important strategy for estimating with fractions is to use Benchmark Values. These are simple fractions with which you are already familiar:

$$\frac{1}{10}, \frac{1}{5}, \frac{1}{4}, \frac{1}{3}, \frac{1}{2}, \frac{2}{3}, \text{ and } \frac{3}{4}$$

You can use Benchmark Values to compare fractions:

$$\text{Which is greater: } \frac{127}{255} \text{ or } \frac{162}{320}?$$

When you find seemingly complicated fractions on the GMAT, use Benchmark Values to make sense of them.

If you recognize that 127 is less than half of 255, and 162 is more than half of 320, you will save yourself a lot of cumbersome computation.

You can also use Benchmark Values to estimate computations involving fractions:

$$\text{What is } \frac{10}{22} \text{ of } \frac{5}{18} \text{ of 2000?}$$

If you recognize that these fractions are very close to the Benchmark Values $\frac{1}{2}$ and $\frac{1}{4}$, you can estimate:

$$\frac{1}{2} \text{ of } \frac{1}{4} \text{ of 2000} = 250. \text{ Therefore, } \frac{10}{22} \text{ of } \frac{5}{18} \text{ of 2000} \approx 250.$$

Notice that the rounding errors compensated for each other.

$\frac{10}{22} \approx \frac{10}{20} = \frac{1}{2}$ You decreased the denominator, so you rounded up: $\frac{10}{22} < \frac{1}{2}$

$\frac{5}{18} \approx \frac{5}{20} = \frac{1}{4}$ You increased the denominator, so you rounded down: $\frac{5}{18} > \frac{1}{4}$

If you had rounded $\frac{5}{18}$ to $\frac{6}{18} = \frac{1}{3}$ instead, then you would have rounded **both** fractions up. This would lead to a slight but systematic overestimation.

$$\frac{1}{2} \times \frac{1}{3} \times 2000 \approx 333$$

Try to make your rounding errors cancel by rounding some numbers up and others down.

*Manhattan*GMAT*Prep
the new standard

Smart Numbers: Multiples of the Denominators

Sometimes, fraction problems on the GMAT include unspecified numerical amounts; often these unspecified amounts are described by variables. In these cases, pick real numbers to stand in for the variables. To make the computation easier, choose **Smart Numbers** equal to common multiples of the denominators of the fractions in the problem.

For example, consider this problem:

> The Crandalls' hot tub is half filled. Their swimming pool, which has a capacity four times that of the tub, is filled to four-fifths of its capacity. If the hot tub is drained into the swimming pool, to what fraction of its capacity will the pool be filled?

The denominators in this problem are 2 and 5. The Smart Number is the least common denominator, which is 10. Therefore, assign the hot tub a capacity of 10 units. Since the swimming pool has a capacity 4 times that of the pool, the swimming pool has a capacity of 40 units. We know that the hot tub is only half-filled; therefore, it has 5 units of water in it. The swimming pool is four-fifths of the way filled, so it has 32 units of water in it.

Let us add the 5 units of water from the hot tub to the 32 units of water that are already in the swimming pool: 32 + 5 = 37.

With 37 units of water and a total capacity of 40, the pool will be filled to $\dfrac{37}{40}$ of its total capacity.

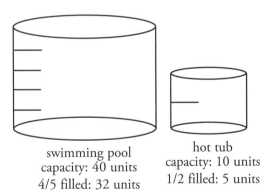

swimming pool
capacity: 40 units
4/5 filled: 32 units

hot tub
capacity: 10 units
1/2 filled: 5 units

You can often use Smart Numbers to help you solve problems with unspecified amounts.

When Not to Use Smart Numbers

In some problems, even though an amount might be unknown to you, it is actually specified in the problem in another way. In these cases, you cannot use Smart Numbers to assign real numbers to the variables. For example, consider this problem:

> Mark's comic book collection contains 1/3 Killer Fish comics and 3/8 Shazaam Woman comics. The remainder of his collection consists of Boom! comics. If Mark has 70 Boom! comics, how many comics does he have in his entire collection?

Even though you do not know the number of comics in Mark's collection, you can see that the total is not completely unspecified. You know a piece of the total: 70 Boom! comics. You can use this information to find the total. Do not use Smart Numbers here. Instead, solve similar problems by figuring out how big the known piece is; then, use that knowledge to find the size of the whole. You will need to set up an equation and solve:

$$\frac{1}{3} \text{ Killer Fish } + \frac{3}{8} \text{ Shazaam Woman} = \frac{17}{24} \text{ comics that are not Boom!}$$

Therefore, $\frac{7}{24}$ of the comics are Boom! comics.

$$\frac{7}{24}x = 70$$

$$x = 70 \times \frac{24}{7}$$

$$x = 240$$

Mark has 240 comics.

In summary, **do** pick smart numbers when no amounts are given in the problem, but **do not** pick smart numbers when <u>any</u> amount or total is given!

If there is even 1 specified amount in a problem, you cannot use Smart Numbers to solve it.

Problem Set

For problems #1–5, decide whether the given operation will yield an INCREASE, a DECREASE, or a result that will STAY THE SAME.

1. Multiply the numerator of a positive, proper fraction by $\frac{3}{2}$.

2. Add 1 to the numerator of a positive, proper fraction and subtract 1 from its denominator.

3. Multiply both the numerator and denominator of a positive, proper fraction by $3\frac{1}{2}$.

4. Multiply a positive, proper fraction by $\frac{3}{8}$.

5. Divide a positive, proper fraction by $\frac{3}{13}$.

Solve problems #6–15.

6. Simplify: $\dfrac{10x}{5 + x}$

7. Simplify: $\dfrac{8(3)(x)^2(3)}{6x}$

8. Simplify: $\dfrac{\dfrac{3}{5} + \dfrac{1}{3}}{\dfrac{2}{3} + \dfrac{2}{5}}$

9. Simplify: $\dfrac{12ab^3 - 6a^2b}{3ab}$ (given that $ab \neq 0$)

10. Put these fractions in order from least to greatest: $\dfrac{9}{17}$ $\dfrac{3}{16}$ $\dfrac{19}{20}$ $\dfrac{7}{15}$

11. Put these fractions in order from least to greatest: $\dfrac{2}{3}$ $\dfrac{3}{13}$ $\dfrac{5}{7}$ $\dfrac{2}{9}$

12. Lisa spends $\dfrac{3}{8}$ of her monthly paycheck on rent and $\dfrac{5}{12}$ on food. Her roommate, Carrie, who earns twice as much as Lisa, spends $\dfrac{1}{4}$ of her monthly paycheck on rent and $\dfrac{1}{2}$ on food. If the two women decide to donate the remainder of their money to charity each month, what fraction of their combined monthly income will they donate?

13.   Rob spends $\frac{1}{2}$ of his monthly paycheck, after taxes, on rent. He spends $\frac{1}{3}$ on food

and $\frac{1}{8}$ on entertainment. If he donates the entire remainder, $500, to charity, what

is Rob's monthly income, after taxes?

14.   Are $\frac{\sqrt{3}}{2}$ and $\frac{2\sqrt{3}}{3}$ reciprocals?

15.   Estimate to the closest integer: What is $\frac{11}{30}$ of $\frac{6}{20}$ of 120?

1. **INCREASE:** Multiplying the numerator of a positive fraction increases the numerator. As the numerator of a positive, proper fraction increases, its value increases.

2. **INCREASE:** As the numerator of a positive, proper fraction increases, the value of the fraction increases. As the denominator of a positive, proper fraction decreases, the value of the fraction also increases. Both actions will work to increase the value of the fraction.

3. **STAY THE SAME:** Multiplying or dividing the numerator and denominator of a fraction by the same number will not change the value of the fraction.

4. **DECREASE:** Multiplying a positive number by a proper fraction decreases the number.

5. **INCREASE:** Dividing a positive number by a positive, proper fraction increases the number.

6. **CANNOT SIMPLIFY:** There is no way to simplify this fraction; it is already in simplest form. Remember, you cannot split the denominator!

7. **12x:** First, cancel terms in both the numerator and the denominator. Then combine terms.

$$\frac{8(3)(x)^2(3)}{6x} = \frac{8(3)(x)^2(3)}{62x} = \frac{84(x)^2(3)}{2x} = \frac{4(x)^2(3)}{x} = 4(x)(3) = 12x$$

8. $\dfrac{7}{8}$ **:** First, add the fractions in the numerator and denominator. This results in $\dfrac{14}{15}$ and $\dfrac{16}{15}$, respectively. To save time, multiply each of the small fractions by 15, which is the common denominator of all the fractions in the problem. Because we are multiplying the numerator *and* the denominator of the whole complex fraction by 15, we are not changing its value.

$$\frac{9+5}{10+6} = \frac{14}{16} = \frac{7}{8}$$

9. **2($2b^2 - a$) or $4b^2 - 2a$:** First, factor out common terms in the numerator. Then, cancel terms in both the numerator and denominator.

$$\frac{6ab(2b^2 - a)}{3ab} = 2(2b^2 - a) \text{ or } 4b^2 - 2a$$

10. $\dfrac{3}{16} < \dfrac{7}{15} < \dfrac{9}{17} < \dfrac{19}{20}$ **:** Use Benchmark Values to compare these fractions.

$\dfrac{9}{17}$ is slightly more than $\dfrac{1}{2}$. $\dfrac{3}{16}$ is slightly less than $\dfrac{1}{4}$.

$\dfrac{19}{20}$ is slightly less than 1. $\dfrac{7}{15}$ is slightly less than $\dfrac{1}{2}$.

This makes it easy to order the fractions: $\dfrac{3}{16} < \dfrac{7}{15} < \dfrac{9}{17} < \dfrac{19}{20}$.

11. $\frac{2}{9} < \frac{3}{13} < \frac{2}{3} < \frac{5}{7}$: Using Benchmark Values, you should notice that $\frac{3}{13}$ and $\frac{2}{9}$ are both less than $\frac{1}{2}$.

$\frac{2}{3}$ and $\frac{5}{7}$ are both more than $\frac{1}{2}$. Use cross–multiplication to compare each pair of fractions:

$$3 \times 9 = 27 \qquad \frac{3}{13} \bowtie \frac{2}{9} \qquad 2 \times 13 = 26 \qquad \frac{3}{13} > \frac{2}{9}$$

$$2 \times 7 = 14 \qquad \frac{2}{3} \bowtie \frac{5}{7} \qquad 5 \times 3 = 15 \qquad \frac{2}{3} < \frac{5}{7}$$

This makes it easy to order the fractions: $\frac{2}{9} < \frac{3}{13} < \frac{2}{3} < \frac{5}{7}$.

12. $\frac{17}{72}$: Use Smart Numbers to solve this problem. Since the denominators in the problem are 8, 12, 4, and 2, assign Lisa a monthly paycheck of $24. Assign her roommate, who earns twice as much, a monthly paycheck of $48. The two women's monthly expenses break down as follows:

	Rent	Food	Leftover
Lisa	$\frac{3}{8}$ of 24 = 9	$\frac{5}{12}$ of 24 = 10	24 − (9 + 10) = 5
Carrie	$\frac{1}{4}$ of 48 = 12	$\frac{1}{2}$ of 48 = 24	48 − (12 + 24) = 12

The women will donate a total of $17, out of their combined monthly income of $72.

13. **$12,000:** You cannot use Smart Numbers in this problem, because the total amount is specified. Even though the exact figure is not given in the problem, a portion of the total is specified. This means that the total is a certain number, although you do not know what it is. In fact, the total is exactly what you are being asked to find. Clearly, if you assign a number to represent the total, you will not be able to accurately find the total.

First, use addition to find the fraction of Rob's money that he spends on rent, food, and entertainment: $\frac{1}{2} + \frac{1}{3} + \frac{1}{8} = \frac{12}{24} + \frac{8}{24} + \frac{3}{24} = \frac{23}{24}$. Therefore, the $500 that he donates to charity represents $\frac{1}{24}$ of his total

monthly paycheck. We can set up a proportion: $\frac{500}{x} = \frac{1}{24}$. Thus, Rob's monthly income is $500 × 24, or $12,000.

14. **YES:** The product of a number and its reciprocal must equal 1. To test whether or not two numbers are reciprocals, multiply them. If the product is 1, they are reciprocals; if it is not, they are not:

$$\frac{\sqrt{3}}{2} \times \frac{2\sqrt{3}}{3} = \frac{2\left(\sqrt{3}\right)^2}{2(3)} = \frac{6}{6} = 1$$

The numbers are indeed reciprocals.

15. **Approximately 13:** Use Benchmark Values to estimate: $\frac{11}{30}$ is slightly more than $\frac{1}{3}$. $\frac{6}{20}$ is slightly less than $\frac{1}{3}$. Therefore, $\frac{11}{30}$ of $\frac{6}{20}$ of 120 should be approximately $\frac{1}{3}$ of $\frac{1}{3}$ of 120, or $\frac{120}{9}$, which is slightly more than 13.

Another technique to solve this problem would be to write the product and cancel common factors:

$$\frac{11}{30} \times \frac{6}{20} \times 120 = \frac{(11)(6)(120)}{(30)(20)} = \frac{(11)(\cancel{6})(120)}{(\cancel{30}5)(20)} = \frac{(11)(\cancel{120}6)}{(5)(\cancel{20})} = \frac{66}{5} = 13.2$$

Note that for estimation problems, there is no "correct" answer. The key is to arrive at an estimate that is close to the exact answer—and to do so quickly!

Chapter 3
of
FRACTIONS, DECIMALS, & PERCENTS

PERCENTS

In This Chapter . . .

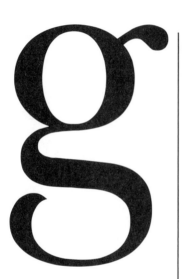

- Percents as Decimals: Multiplication Shortcut
- Percents as Fractions: The Percent Table
- Benchmark Values: 10%
- Percent Increase and Decrease
- Percent Change vs. Percent of Original
- Successive Percents
- Smart Numbers: Pick 100
- Interest Formulas
- Chemical Mixtures

PERCENTS

The other major way to express a part–whole relationship (in addition to decimals and fractions) is to use percents. Percent literally means "per one hundred." One can conceive of percent as simply a special type of fraction or decimal that involves the number 100.

> 75% of the students like chocolate ice cream.

This means that, out of every 100 students, 75 like chocolate ice cream.

In fraction form, we write this as $\frac{75}{100}$, which simplifies to $\frac{3}{4}$.

In decimal form, we write this as 0.75 or seventy–five hundredths. Note that the last digit of the percent is in the hundredths place value.

One common mistake is the belief that 100% equals 100. This is not correct. In fact, 100% means $\frac{100}{100}$, or one hundred hundredths. Therefore, 100% = 1.

Percent problems occur frequently on the GMAT. The key to these percent problems is to make them concrete by picking real numbers with which to work.

> A percent is simply a fraction with a denominator of 100.

Percents as Decimals: Multiplication Shortcut

One way of working with percents is by converting them into decimals. Percents can be converted into decimals by moving the decimal point 2 spaces to the left.

70.7% = 0.707	75% = 0.75	70% = 0.70 = 0.7	7% = 0.07	0.7% = 0.007
80.8% = 0.808	88% = 0.88	80% = 0.80 = 0.8	8% = 0.08	0.8% = 0.008

A decimal can be converted into a percentage by moving the decimal point two spaces to the right. For example:

0.6 = 60%	0.28 = 28%	0.459 = 45.9%	0.3041 = 30.41%

Remember, the percentage is always bigger than the decimal!

Note that there are numbers greater than 100%. If 100% = 1, consider the following:

2 = 200%	3 = 300%	4.1 = 410%	5.68 = 568%

Changing percents into decimals is one fast way to solve "percent of" problems.

> What is 65% of 500?

The phrase "percent of" (% of) signals multiplication. "Is" means "equals," of course. So we have $x = 0.65(500) = 325.00 = 325$.

PERCENTS STRATEGY

Percents as Fractions: The Percent Table

A simple but useful way of structuring basic percent problems on the GMAT is by relating percents to fractions through a percent table as shown below.

	Numbers	Percentage Fraction
PART		
WHOLE		100

A PART is some PERCENT of a WHOLE.

$$\frac{PART}{WHOLE} = \frac{PERCENT}{100}$$

Example 1:   What is 30% of 80?

Be careful that you have correctly identified the part and the whole when setting up your percent table.

We are given the whole and the percent, and we are looking for the part. First, we fill in the percent table. Then we set up a proportion, cancel, cross–multiply, and solve:

	Numbers	Percentage Fraction
PART	x	30
WHOLE	80	100

$$\frac{x}{80} = \frac{3\cancel{0}}{10\cancel{0}} = \frac{3}{10} \qquad 10x = 240 \qquad x = 24$$

We can also solve this problem using decimal equivalents: $(0.30)(80) = (3)(8) = 24$

Example 2:   75% of what number is 21?

We are given the part and the percent, and we are looking for the whole. First, we fill in the percent table. Then we set up a proportion, cancel, cross–multiply, and solve:

	Numbers	Percentage Fraction
PART	21	75
WHOLE	x	100

$$\frac{21}{x} = \frac{\cancel{75}}{\cancel{100}} = \frac{3}{4} \qquad 3x = 84 \qquad x = 28$$

Likewise, we can also solve this problem using decimal equivalents:

$$(0.75)x = 21 \quad \text{then move the decimal} \rightarrow \quad 75x = 2,100 \qquad x = 28$$

Example 3:   90 is what percent of 40?

We are given the part and the whole, and we are looking for the percent. Note that the "part" (90) is BIGGER than the "whole" (40). That is okay. Just make sure that you are taking the percent OF the "whole." Here, we are taking a percent OF 40, so 40 is the "whole."

First, we fill in the percent table. Then we set up a proportion again and solve:

	Numbers	Percentage Fraction
PART	90	x
WHOLE	40	100

$$\frac{\cancel{90}}{\cancel{40}} = \frac{9}{4} = \frac{x}{100} \qquad 4x = 900 \qquad x = 225$$

90 is 225% of 40. Notice that you wind up with a percent BIGGER than 100%. That is what you should expect when the "part" is bigger than the "whole."

Benchmark Values: 10%

To find 10% of any number, just move the decimal point to the left one place.

10% of 500 is 50   10% of 34.99 = 3.499   10% of 0.978 is 0.0978

You can use the Benchmark Value of 10% to estimate percents. For example:

> Karen bought a new television, originally priced at $690. However, she had
> a coupon that saved her $67. For what percent discount was Karen's
> coupon?

You know that 10% of 690 would be 69. Therefore, 67 is slightly less than 10% of 690.

Percent Increase and Decrease

Some percent problems involve the concept of percent change. For example:

> The price of a cup of coffee increased from 80 cents to 84 cents. By what
> percent did the price change?

Percent change problems can be solved using our handy percent table, with a small adjustment. The price change (84 − 80 = 4 cents) is considered the part, while the *original* price (80 cents) is considered the whole.

CHANGE	4	x
ORIGINAL	80	100

$$\frac{\text{CHANGE}}{\text{ORIGINAL}} = \frac{\text{PERCENT}}{100}$$

$$\frac{\cancel{4}}{\cancel{80}} = \frac{1}{20} = \frac{x}{100} \qquad 20x = 100 \qquad x = 5 \quad \text{Thus, the price increased by 5\%.}$$

By the way, do not forget to divide by the original! The percent change is NOT 4%, which may be a wrong answer choice.

Alternatively, a question might be phrased as follows:

> If the price of a $30 shirt decreased by 20%, what was the final price of the
> shirt?

The whole is the original price of the shirt. The percent change is 20%. In order to find the answer, we must first find the part, which is the amount of the decrease:

CHANGE	x	20
ORIGINAL	30	100

$$\frac{x}{30} = \frac{\cancel{20}}{\cancel{100}} = \frac{1}{5} \qquad 5x = 30 \qquad x = 6$$

Therefore, the price of the shirt decreased by $6. The final price of the shirt was $30 − $6 = $24.

> The whole is the original value. It is not necessarily the largest number in the problem.

*Manhattan*GMAT*Prep

Percent Change vs. Percent of Original

Looking back at the cup of coffee problem, we see that the new price (84 cents) was higher than the original price (80 cents).

We can ask what percent OF the original price is represented by the new price.

$$\frac{\cancel{84}}{\cancel{80}} = \frac{21}{20} = \frac{x}{100} \qquad 20x = 2,100 \qquad x = 105$$

Thus, the new price is 105% OF the original price. Remember that the percent CHANGE is 5%. That is, the new price is 5% HIGHER THAN the original price. There is a fundamental relationship between these numbers, resulting from the simple idea that the CHANGE equals the NEW value minus the ORIGINAL value, or equivalently, ORIGINAL + CHANGE = NEW:

If a quantity is increased by x percent, then the new quantity is $(100 + x)$% OF the original. Thus a 15% increase produces a quantity that is 115% OF the original.

We can write this relationship thus: $\text{ORIGINAL} \times \left(1 + \dfrac{\text{Percent Increase}}{100}\right) = \text{NEW}$

In the case of the cup of coffee, we see that $80 \times \left(1 + \dfrac{5}{100}\right) = 80\,(1.05) = 84$.

Likewise, in the shirt problem, we had a 20% decrease in the price of a \$30 shirt, resulting in a new price of \$24.

The new price is some percent OF the old price. Let us calculate that percent.

$$\frac{\cancel{24}}{\cancel{30}} = \frac{4}{5} = \frac{x}{100} \qquad 5x = 400 \qquad x = 80$$

Thus, the new price (20% LESS THAN the original price) is 80% OF the original price.

If a quantity is decreased by x percent, then the new quantity is $(100 - x)$% OF the original. Thus a 15% decrease produces a quantity that is 85% OF the original.

We can write this relationship thus: $\text{ORIGINAL} \times \left(1 - \dfrac{\text{Percent Decrease}}{100}\right) = \text{NEW}$.

In the case of the shirt, we see that $30 \times \left(1 - \dfrac{20}{100}\right) = 30\,(0.80) = 24$.

These formulas are all just another way of saying $\text{ORIGINAL} \pm \text{CHANGE} = \text{NEW}$.

Manhattan **GMAT** *Prep*
the new standard

(side note) 100% plus or minus a percent change equals the percent OF the original quantity that the new quantity represents.

Example 4:   What number is 50% greater than 60?

The whole is the original value, which is 60. The percent change (i.e., the percent "greater than") is 50%. In order to find the answer, we must first find the part, which is the amount of the increase:

CHANGE	x	50
ORIGINAL	60	100

$$\frac{x}{60} = \frac{\cancel{50}}{\cancel{100}} = \frac{1}{2} \qquad 2x = 60 \qquad x = 30$$

We know that $\text{ORIGINAL} \pm \text{CHANGE} = \text{NEW}$. Therefore, the number that is 50% greater than 60 is $60 + 30 = 90$, which is 150% of 60.

We could also solve this problem using the formula :

$$\text{ORIGINAL} \times \left(1 + \frac{\text{Percent Increase}}{100}\right) = \text{NEW} \qquad 60\left(1 + \frac{50}{100}\right) = 60(1.5) = 90$$

Be especially careful of percent change problems where the percent change is greater than 100%.

Example 5:   What number is 150% greater than 60?

The whole is the original value, which is 60. The percent change (i.e., the percent "greater than") is 150%. In order to find the answer, we must first find the part, which is the amount of the increase:

CHANGE	x	150
ORIGINAL	60	100

$$\frac{x}{60} = \frac{\cancel{150}}{\cancel{100}} = \frac{3}{2} \qquad 2x = 180 \qquad x = 90$$

Now, x is the CHANGE, NOT the new value! **It is easy to forget to add back the original amount when the percent change is more than 100%.** Thus, the number that is 150% greater than 60 is $60 + 90 = 150$, which is 250% of 60.

We could also solve this problem using the formula :

$$\text{ORIGINAL} \times \left(1 + \frac{\text{Percent Increase}}{100}\right) = \text{NEW} \qquad 60\left(1 + \frac{150}{100}\right) = 60(2.5) = 150$$

For Data Sufficiency problems, all you need to compute a percent change is the RATIO of Change to Original. You do not need the actual values. In fact, because Original + Change = New, **you can compute the percent change using the ratio of ANY TWO of the following: Original, Change, and New.**

By what percent did the price of a book increase?

(1) The ratio of the book's original price to its new price is 4 : 5.
(2) The ratio of the change in the book's price to its new price is 1 : 5.

Either statement indicates a 25% increase in price, as you can see by picking numbers ($4 for the original price, $1 for the change, and $5 for the new price). The correct answer is (D): EITHER statement is sufficient to answer the question.

*Manhattan*GMAT*Prep
the new standard

Successive Percents

One of the GMAT's favorite tricks involves successive percents.

> If a ticket increased in price by 20%, and then increased again by 5%, by what percent did the ticket price increase in total?

Although it may seem counter–intuitive, the answer is NOT 25%.

To understand why, consider a concrete example. Let us say that the ticket initially cost $100. After increasing by 20%, the ticket price went up to $120 ($20 is 20% of $100).

Here is where it gets tricky. The ticket price goes up again by 5%. However, it increases by 5% of the **NEW PRICE** of $120 (not 5% of the *original* $100 price). 5% of $120 is $0.05(120) = \$6$. Therefore, the final price of the ticket is $120 + $6 = $126.

You can now see that two successive percent increases, the first of 20% and the second of 5%, DO NOT result in a combined 25% increase. In fact, they result in a combined 26% increase (because the ticket price increased from $100 to $126).

Successive percents CANNOT simply be added together! This holds for successive increases, successive decreases, and for combinations of increases and decreases. If a ticket goes up in price by 30% and then goes down by 10%, the price has NOT in fact gone up a net of 20%. Likewise, if an index increases by 15% and then falls by 15%, it does NOT return to its original value! (Try it—you will see that the index is down 2.25% overall.)

A great way to solve successive percent problems is to choose real numbers and see what happens. The preceding example used the real value of $100 for the initial price of the ticket, making it easy to see exactly what happened to the ticket price with each increase. **Usually, 100 will be the easiest real number to choose for percent problems.**

Increasing a price by 20% is the same as multiplying the price by 1.20.
Increasing the new price by 5% is the same as multiplying that new price by 1.05.
Thus, you can also write the relationship this way:

$$\text{ORIGINAL} \times (1.20) \times (1.05) = \text{FINAL PRICE}$$

When you multiply 1.20 by 1.05, you get 1.26, indicating that the price increased by 26% overall.

This approach works well for problems that involve many successive steps (e.g., compound interest). However, in the end, it is still usually best to pick $100 for the original price and solve using concrete numbers.

Smart Numbers: Pick 100

More often than not, percent problems on the GMAT include unspecified numerical amounts; often these unspecified amounts are described by variables.

> A shirt that initially cost *d* dollars was on sale for 20% off. If *s* represents the sale price of the shirt, *d* is what percentage of *s*?

This is an easy problem that might look confusing. To solve percent problems such as this one, simply pick 100 for the unspecified amount (just as we did when solving successive percents).

If the shirt initially cost $100, then *d* = 100. If the shirt was on sale for 20% off, then the new price of the shirt is $80. Thus, *s* = 80.

The question asks: *d* is what percentage of *s*, or 100 is what percentage of 80? Using a percent table, we fill in 80 as the whole and 100 as the part (even though the part happens to be larger than the whole in this case). We are looking for the percent, so we set up a proportion, cross–multiply, and solve:

In a percent problem with unspecified amounts, pick 100 to represent the original value.

PART	100	*x*
WHOLE	80	100

$$\frac{100}{80} = \frac{x}{100} \qquad 80x = 10{,}000 \qquad x = 125$$

Therefore, *d* is 125% of *s*.

The important point here is that, like successive percent problems and other percent problems that include unspecified amounts, this example is most easily solved by plugging in a real value. For percent problems, the easiest value to plug in is generally 100. **The fastest way to success with GMAT percent problems with unspecified amounts is to pick 100.**

Interest Formulas

Certain GMAT percent problems require a working knowledge of basic interest formulas. The compound interest formula, relatively rare on the GMAT, may look complicated, but it just expresses the idea of "successive percents" for a number of periods.

	Formula	**Example**
SIMPLE INTEREST	Principal × Rate × Time	$5,000 invested for 6 months at an annual rate of 7% will earn $175 in simple interest. Principal = $5,000, Rate = 7% or 0.07, Time = 6 months or 0.5 years. ***Prt* = $5,000(0.07)(0.5) = $175**
COMPOUND INTEREST	$P(1 + \frac{r}{n})^{nt}$, where *P* = principal, *r* = rate (decimal) *n* = **number of times per year** *t* = **number of years**	$5,000 invested for 1 year at a rate of 8% compounded quarterly will earn approximately $412: **$5,000$\left(1 + \frac{0.08}{4}\right)^{4(1)}$ = $5,412**

Chemical Mixtures

Another type of GMAT percent problem bears mention: the chemical mixture problem.

> A 500 mL solution is 20% alcohol by volume. If 100 mL of water is added, what is the new concentration of alcohol, as a percent of volume?

Chemical mixture problems can be solved systematically by using a mixture chart.

Set up a mixture chart with the substance labels in rows and "Original," "Change" and "New" in the columns. This way, you can keep careful track of the various components and their changes.

Volume (mL)	ORIGINAL	CHANGE	NEW
Alcohol			
Water			
Total Solution			

Note that Original + Change = New. Moreover, the rows contain the parts of the mixture and sum to a total. Only insert actual amounts; compute percents off on the side.

First, fill in the amounts that you know. We put 500 mL of solution in the Original column. We also put +100 mL of water in the Change column. Since no alcohol was added or removed, we put 0 mL of alcohol in the Change column. This tells us that our total Change is 100 mL as well. You do not need to input the units (mL).

Volume (mL)	ORIGINAL	CHANGE	NEW
Alcohol		0	
Water		+100	
Total Solution	500	+100	

Since the Original solution is 20% alcohol, we can compute the ml of alcohol in the Original solution by asking: How many ml of alcohol is 20% of 500 mL? Let us solve this using the decimal equivalent: $x = (0.20)(500 \text{ mL}) = 100 \text{ mL}$

Now, fill in all the remaining numbers.

Volume (mL)	ORIGINAL	CHANGE	NEW
Alcohol	100	0	100
Water	400	+100	500
Total Solution	500	+100	600

Finally, we can find the new alcohol percentage: $\dfrac{\text{Alcohol}}{\text{Total}} = \dfrac{100}{600} = \dfrac{1}{6} \approx 0.167 = 16.7\%$.

Note that with this chart, you can handle proportions of many kinds. For instance, you might have been asked the concentration of water in the final solution. Simply take the quantities from the proper rows and columns and calculate a proportion.

Problem Set

Solve the following problems. Use a percent table to organize percent problems, and pick 100 when dealing with unspecified amounts.

1. x% of y is 10. y% of 120 is 48. What is x?

2.   A stereo was marked down by 30% and sold for $84. What was the presale price of the stereo?

3.   From 1980 to 1990, the population of Mitannia increased by 6%. From 1991 to 2000, it decreased by 3%. What was the overall percentage change in the population of Mitannia from 1980 to 2000?

4.   If y is decreased by 20% and then increased by 60%, what is the new number, expressed in terms of y?

5.   A 7% car loan, which is compounded annually, has an interest payment of $210 after the first year. What is the principal on the loan?

6.   A bowl was half full of water. 4 cups of water were then added to the bowl, filling the bowl to 70% of its capacity. How many cups of water are now in the bowl?

7.   A large tub is filled with 920 units of alcohol and 1,800 units of water. 40% of the water evaporates. What percent of the remaining liquid is water?

8. x is 40% of y. 50% of y is 40. 16 is what percent of x?

9.   800, increased by 50% and then decreased by 30%, yields what number?

10. Lori deposits $100 in a savings account at 2% interest, compounded annually. After 3 years, what is the balance on the account? (Assume Lori makes no withdrawals or deposits.)

11. A full bottle contains 40% oil, 20% vinegar, and 40% water. The bottle is poured into a larger bottle, four times as big as the original. The remaining space in the larger bottle is then filled with water. If there were 8 mL of oil in the original bottle, how much water is in the final mixture?

12. If 1,600 is increased by 20%, and then reduced by y%, yielding 1,536, what is y?

13.   A certain copy machine is set to reduce an image by 13%. If Steve photocopies a document on this machine, and then photocopies the copy on the same machine, what percent of the original will his final image size be?

14.   A bottle is 80% full. The liquid in the bottle consists of 60% guava juice and 40% pineapple juice. The remainder of the bottle is then filled with 70 mL of rum. How much guava juice is in the bottle?

The following problem is a Data Sufficiency question.

15.   Company Z only sells chairs and tables. What percent of its revenue in 2008 did Company Z derive from its sales of tables?

       (1) In 2008, the average price of tables sold by Company Z was 10% higher than the average price of chairs sold by Company Z

       (2) In 2008, Company Z sold 20% fewer tables than chairs.

1. **25:** We can use two percent tables to solve this problem. Begin with the fact that $y\%$ of 120 is 48:

PART	48	y
WHOLE	120	100

$4,800 = 120y$
$y = 40$

Then, set up a percent table for the fact that $x\%$ of 40 is 10.

PART	10	x
WHOLE	40	100

$1,000 = 40x$
$x = 25$

We can also set up equations with decimal equivalents to solve:

$(0.01y)(120) = 48$, so $1.2y = 48$ or $y = 40$. Therefore, since we know that $(0.01x)(y) = 10$, we have:

$(0.01x)(40) = 10$ $40x = 1,000$ $x = 25$.

2. **$120:** We can use a percent table to solve this problem. Remember that the stereo was marked down 30% from the original, so we have to solve for the original price.

CHANGE	x	30
ORIGINAL	$84 + x$	100

$\dfrac{x}{84 + x} = \dfrac{30}{100}$ $100x = 30(84 + x)$ $100x = 30(84) + 30x$

$70x = 30(84)$ $x = 36$

Therefore, the original price was $(84 + 36) = \$120$.

We could also solve this problem using the formula : $\text{ORIGINAL} \times \left(1 - \dfrac{\text{Percent Decrease}}{100}\right) = \text{NEW}$

$x\left(1 - \dfrac{30}{100}\right) = 84$ $0.7x = 84$ $x = 120$

3. **2.82% increase:** For percent problems, the Smart Number is 100. Therefore, assume that the population of Mitannia in 1980 was 100. Then, apply the successive percents to find the overall percent change:

From 1980–1990, there was a 6% increase: $100(1 + 0.06) = 100(1.06) = 106$
From 1991–2000, there was a 3% decrease: $106(1 - 0.03) = 106(0.97) = 102.82$
Overall, the population increased from 100 to 102.82, representing a 2.82% increase.

4. **1.28y:** For percent problems, the Smart Number is 100. Therefore, assign y a value of 100. Then, apply the successive percent to find the overall percentage change:

(1) y is decreased by 20%: $100(1 - 0.20) = 100(0.8) = 80$
(2) Then, it is increased by 60%: $80(1 + 0.60) = 80(1.6) = 128$
Overall, there was a 28% increase. If the original value of y is 100, the new value is $1.28y$.

5. **$3,000:** We can use a percent table to solve this problem, which helps us find the decimal equivalent equation.

PART	210	7
WHOLE	x	100

$21,000 = 7x$
$x = 3,000$

6. **14:** There are some problems for which you cannot use Smart Numbers, since the total amount can be calculated. This is one of those problems. Instead, use a percent table:

PART	$0.5x + 4$	70
WHOLE	x	100

$$\frac{0.5x + 4}{x} = \frac{70}{100} = \frac{7}{10}$$

$$5x + 40 = 7x$$
$$40 = 2x$$
$$x = 20$$

The capacity of the bowl is 20 cups. There are 14 cups in the bowl {70% of 20, or 0.5(20) + 4}.

PART	4	20
WHOLE	x	100

Alternately, the 4 cups added to the bowl represent 20% of the total capacity. Use a percent table to solve for x, the whole. Since $x = 20$, there are 14 (50% of 20 + 4) cups in the bowl.

7. **54%:** For this liquid mixture problem, set up a table with two columns: one for the original mixture and one for the mixture after the water evaporates from the tub.

	Original	After Evaporation
Alcohol	920	920
Water	1,800	$0.60(1,800) = 1,080$
TOTAL	2,720	2,000

The remaining liquid in the tub is $\frac{1,080}{2,000}$, or 54%, water.

We could also solve for the new amount of water using the formula:

$$\text{ORIGINAL} \times \left(1 - \frac{\text{Percent Decrease}}{100}\right) = \text{NEW}$$

$$1,800\left(1 - \frac{40}{100}\right) = (1,800)(0.6) = 1,080 \text{ units of water. Water is } \frac{1,080}{920 + 1,080} = \frac{1,080}{2,000} = 54\% \text{ of the total.}$$

8. **50%:** Use two percent tables to solve this problem. Begin with the fact that 50% of y is 40:

PART	40	50
WHOLE	y	100

$$4,000 = 50y$$
$$y = 80$$

Then, set up a percent table for the fact that x is 40% of y.

PART	x	40
WHOLE	80	100

$$3,200 = 100x$$
$$x = 32$$

Finally, 16 is 50% of 32. We could alternatively set up equations with decimal equivalents to solve: $x = (0.4)y$ We also know that $(0.5)y = 40$, =so $y = 80$ and $x = (0.4)(80) = 32$. Therefore, 16 is half, or 50%, of x.

9. **840:** Apply the successive percent to find the overall percentage change:
    (1) 800 is increased by 50%: $800 \times 1.5 = 1,200$
    (2) Then, the result is decreased by 30%: $1,200 \times 0.7 = 840$

10. **$106.12:** Interest compounded annually is just a series of successive percents:
   (1) 100.00 is increased by 2%: $100(1.02) = 102$
   (2) 102.00 is increased by 2%: $102(1.02) = 104.04$
   (3) 104.04 is increased by 2%: $104.04(1.02) \cong 106.12$

11. **68 mL:** First, organize the information for the original situation:
   8 mL = 40% oil x mL = 20% vinegar y mL = 40% water

There is the same amount of water in the original as there is oil. So, $y = 8$ mL. If you know that 8 mL is 40% of the total, then 20%, or x, must be half as much, or 4 mL. The original solution contains 20 mL of liquid all together.

Volume (mL)	ORIGINAL	CHANGE	NEW
Oil	8		
Vinegar	4		
Water	8		
TOTAL	20		

Then, the solution is poured into a new bottle with a capacity of 80 mL (4 × 20). The remaining space, 60 mL, is filled with water. Therefore, there are 68 mL of water in the final solution (8 from the original mixture and 60 added into the larger bottle).

Volume (mL)	ORIGINAL	CHANGE	NEW
Oil	8	0	8
Vinegar	4	0	4
Water	8	60	68
TOTAL	20	60	80

12. **20:** Apply the percents in succession with two percent tables.

PART	x	120
WHOLE	1,600	100

$192,000 = 100x$
$x = 1,920$

Then, fill in the "change" for the part (1,920 − 1,536 = 384) and the original for the whole (1,920).

PART	384	y
WHOLE	1,920	100

$1,920y = 38,400$
$y = 20$

Alternatively we could solve for the new number using formulas. Because this is a successive percents problem, we need to "chain" the formula: once to reflect the initial increase in the number, then twice to reflect the subsequent decrease:

$$\text{ORIGINAL} \times \left(1 + \frac{\text{Percent Increase}}{100} \right) \times \left(1 - \frac{\text{Percent Decrease}}{100} \right) = \text{NEW}$$

$$1,600 \times \left(1 + \frac{20}{100} \right) \times \left(1 - \frac{y}{100} \right) = 1,536 \qquad 1,920 \times \left(1 - \frac{y}{100} \right) = 1,536 \qquad 1,920 - \frac{1,920y}{100} = 1,536$$

$$1,920 - 1,536 = 19.2\,y \qquad 384 = 19.2\,y \qquad 20 = y$$

13. **75.69%:** This is a series of successive percents. Use Smart Numbers to assign the original document an area of 100 square units.

$$87\% \text{ of } 100 = 0.87 \times 100 = 87$$
$$87\% \text{ of } 87 = 0.87 \times 87 = 75.69$$

14. **168 mL:** If the bottle is 80% full, then the 70 mL of rum represents the empty 20%. Use your knowledge of percents to figure out that 80% is four times as big as 20%. Therefore, there must be $4 \times 70 = 280\,\text{mL}$ of the guava–pineapple mixture in the bottle. (In other words, $0.2x = 70\,\text{mL}$, where x is the capacity of the bottle. Thus $x = 350\,\text{mL}$ and the guava–pineapple mixture is $350\,\text{mL} - 70\,\text{mL} = 280\,\text{mL}$.) Use a percent table to find the amount of guava juice.

PART	x	60
WHOLE	280	100

$$16{,}800 = 100x$$
$$x = 168$$

We can also set up equations with decimal equivalents to solve: $(0.6)(280) = x$, so $168 = x$.

15. **C:** BOTH statements TOGETHER are SUFFICIENT to answer the question. This problem requires that you apply the principle that Price × Quantity = Revenue. (For more on this principle, see Chapter 1 of the *Word Translations* Strategy Guide.) In other respects, however, this problem is like a mixture problem, since there are only two components of Company Z's sales: chairs and tables. Set up a chart as follows, and pick Smart Numbers for the price and quantity for ONE of the items only: say, the chairs.

	Price	Quantity	Revenue
Chairs	$10	100	$1,000
Tables			
TOTAL			

Now fill the chart using the statements:

Statement (1): INSUFFICIENT. We can compute the price of tables, which is 10% higher than $10.

	Price	Quantity	Revenue
Chairs	$10	100	$1,000
Tables	$11		
TOTAL			

We do not have the table quantity, so we cannot find the percent of revenue derived from the tables.

Statement (2): INSUFFICIENT. We can compute the quantity of tables, which is 20% smaller than the quantity of chairs.

	Price	Quantity	Revenue
Chairs	$10	100	$1,000
Tables		80	
TOTAL			

*ManhattanGMAT*Prep
the new standard

We do not have the table price, so we cannot find the percent of revenue derived from the tables.

Statements (1) and (2) TOGETHER: SUFFICIENT.

	Price	Quantity	Revenue
Chairs	$10	100	$1,000
Tables	$11	80	$880
TOTAL			$1,880

Now, in theory, we can compute $880 ÷ $1,880 as a percent. However, you should NOT compute this number! It suffices to know that you <u>can</u> compute it.

Chapter 4
of

FRACTIONS, DECIMALS, & PERCENTS

FDPs

In This Chapter . . .

- FDP Connections
- Converting Among Fractions, Decimals, and Percents
- Common FDP Equivalents
- When To Use Which Form
- FDPs and Word Translations

FDP CONNECTIONS

GMAT problems often do not test fractions, decimals, and percents in isolation. Instead, many problems that test your understanding of non-integer numbers involve some kind of combination of fractions, decimals, and percents.

For this reason, we refer to these problems as FDPs (an abbreviation for fraction–decimal–percent). In order to achieve success with FDP problems on the GMAT, you must understand the connections between fractions, decimals, and percents; you should be able to shift amongst the three comfortably and quickly. In a very real sense, fractions, decimals, and percents are three different ways of expressing the exact same thing: a part–whole relationship.

> A **fraction** expresses a part–whole relationship in terms of a numerator (the part) and a denominator (the whole).

> A **decimal** expresses a part–whole relationship in terms of place value (a tenth, a hundredth, a thousandth, etc.).

> A **percent** expresses the special part–whole relationship between a number (the part) and one hundred (the whole).

Fractions, decimals, and percents are all different ways of expressing the same relationship.

Converting Among Fractions, Decimals, and Percents

The following chart reviews the ways to convert from fractions to decimals, from decimals to fractions, from fractions to percents, from percents to fractions, from decimals to percents, and from percents to decimals.

TO → FROM ↓	FRACTION $\frac{3}{8}$	DECIMAL 0.375	PERCENT 37.5%
FRACTION $\frac{3}{8}$		Divide the numerator by the denominator: $3 \div 8 = 0.375$ Use long division if necessary.	Divide the numerator by the denominator and move the decimal two places to the right: $3 \div 8 = 0.375 \rightarrow 37.5\%$
DECIMAL 0.375	Use the place value of the last digit in the decimal as the denominator, and put the decimal's digits in the numerator. Then simplify: $\frac{375}{1000} = \frac{3}{8}$		Move the decimal point two places to the right: $0.375 \rightarrow 37.5\%$
PERCENT 37.5%	Use the digits of the percent for the numerator and 100 for the denominator. Then simplify: $\frac{37.5}{100} = \frac{3}{8}$	Find the percent's decimal point and move it two places to the left: $37.5\% \rightarrow 0.375$	

Common FDP Equivalents

You should memorize the following common equivalents:

Memorize these equivalents so you will recognize them quickly on the test.

Fraction	Decimal	Percent
$1/100$	0.01	1%
$1/50$	0.02	2%
$1/25$	0.04	4%
$1/20$	0.05	5%
$1/10$	0.10	10%
$1/9$	$0.\overline{11} \approx 0.111$	$\approx 11.1\%$
$1/8$	0.125	12.5%
$1/6$	$0.1\overline{6} \approx 0.167$	$\approx 16.7\%$
$1/5$	0.2	20%
$1/4$	0.25	25%
$3/10$	0.3	30%
$1/3$	$0.\overline{3} \approx 0.333$	$\approx 33.3\%$
$3/8$	0.375	37.5%
$2/5$	0.4	40%
$1/2$	0.5	50%

Fraction	Decimal	Percent
$3/5$	0.6	60%
$5/8$	0.625	62.5%
$2/3$	$0.\overline{6} \approx 0.667$	$\approx 66.7\%$
$7/10$	0.7	70%
$3/4$	0.75	75%
$4/5$	0.8	80%
$5/6$	$0.8\overline{3} \approx 0.833$	$\approx 83.3\%$
$7/8$	0.875	87.5%
$9/10$	0.9	90%
$1/1$	1	100%
$5/4$	1.25	125%
$4/3$	$1.\overline{3} \approx 1.33$	133%
$3/2$	1.5	150%
$7/4$	1.75	175%

When To Use Which Form

Fractions are good for cancelling factors in multiplications. They are also the best way of exactly expressing proportions that do not have clean decimal equivalents, such as 1/7. Switch to fractions if there is a handy fractional equivalent of the decimal or percent and/or you think you can cancel lots of factors.

> What is 37.5% of 240?

If you simply convert the percent to a decimal and multiply, you will have to do a fair bit of arithmetic:

$$\begin{array}{r} 0.375 \\ \times\ 240 \\ \hline 0 \\ 15000 \\ 75000 \\ \hline 90.000 \end{array}$$

Alternatively, you can recognize that $0.375 = \dfrac{3}{8}$.

So we have $(0.375)(240) = \left(\dfrac{3}{\cancel{8}}\right)\left(\cancel{240}\,30\right) = 3(30) = 90$.

This is much faster!

Use fractions to cancel factors. Use decimals or percents to estimate or compare quantities.

> A dress is marked up $16\dfrac{2}{3}\%$ to a final price of \$140. What is the original price of the dress?

From the previous page, we know that $16\dfrac{2}{3}\%$ is equivalent to $\dfrac{1}{6}$. Thus, adding $\dfrac{1}{6}$ of a number to itself is the same thing as multiplying by $1 + \dfrac{1}{6} = \dfrac{7}{6}$:

$$\dfrac{7}{6}x = 140 \qquad x = \left(\dfrac{6}{7}\right)140 = \left(\dfrac{6}{\cancel{7}}\right)\cancel{140}\,20 = 120.$$ The original price is \$120.

Decimals, on the other hand, are good for estimating results or for comparing sizes. The reason is that the basis of comparison is equivalent (there is no denominator). The same holds true for **percents**. The implied denominator is always 100, so you can easily compare percents (of the same whole) to each other.

To convert certain fractions to decimals or percents, multiply top and bottom by the same number:

$$\dfrac{17}{25} = \dfrac{17 \times 4}{25 \times 4} = \dfrac{68}{100} = 0.68 = 68\%$$

This process is faster than long division, but it only works when the denominator has only 2's and/or 5's as factors.

In some cases, you might find it easier to compare a bunch of fractions by giving them all a common denominator, rather than by converting them all to decimals or percents. The general rule is this: **prefer fractions for doing multiplication or division, but prefer decimals and percents for doing addition or subtraction, for estimating numbers, or for comparing numbers**.

FDPs and Word Translations

Fractions, decimals, and percents show up in many Word Translation problems. Make sure that you understand and can apply the very common translations below.

In the Problem	Translation
X percent	$\dfrac{X}{100}$
of	Multiply
of Z	Z is the Whole
Y is X percent of Z	Y is the Part, and Z is the Whole
	$Y = \left(\dfrac{X}{100}\right)Z$
	$\text{Part} = \left(\dfrac{\text{Percent}}{100}\right) \times \text{Whole}$
Y is X percent of Z	Alternative: $\dfrac{Y}{Z} = \dfrac{X}{100}$
	$\dfrac{\text{Part}}{\text{Whole}} = \dfrac{\text{Percent}}{100}$
A is $\dfrac{1}{6}$ of B	$A = \left(\dfrac{1}{6}\right)B$
C is 20% of D	$C = (0.20)D$
E is 10% greater than F	$E = (1.10)F$
G is 30% less than H	$G = (100\% - 30\%)H = (0.70)H$
The dress cost J. Then it was marked up 25% and sold.	$\text{Profit} = \text{Revenue} - \text{Cost}$
What is the profit?	$\text{Profit} = (1.25)J - J$ $\text{Profit} = (0.25)J$

Problem Set

1. Express the following as fractions: 2.45   0.008

2. Express the following as fractions: 420%   8%

3. Express the following as decimals: $\dfrac{9}{2}$ $\dfrac{3,000}{10,000}$

4. Express the following as decimals: $1\dfrac{27}{4}$ $12\dfrac{8}{3}$

5. Express the following as percents: $\dfrac{1,000}{10}$ $\dfrac{25}{9}$

6. Express the following as percents: 80.4   0.0007

7. Order from least to greatest: $\dfrac{8}{18}$ 0.8   40%

8. Order from least to greatest: 1.19 $\dfrac{120}{84}$ 131.44%

9. Order from least to greatest: $2\dfrac{4}{7}$ 2400%   2.401

10. Order from least to greatest ($x \neq 0$): $\dfrac{50}{17}x^2$ $2.9x^2$ $(x^2)(3.10\%)$

11. Order from least to greatest: $\dfrac{500}{199}$ 248,000%   2.9002003

12. What number is 62.5% of 192?

13. 200 is 16% of what number?

For problems #14–15, express your answer in terms of the variables given (X, Y, and possibly Z).

14. What number is X percent of Y?

15. X is what percent of Y?

1. To convert a decimal to a fraction, write it over the appropriate power of ten and simplify.

$$2.45 = 2\,\frac{45}{100} = \mathbf{2\,\frac{9}{20}}\ (\text{mixed}) = \mathbf{\frac{49}{20}}\ (\text{improper})$$

$$0.008 = \frac{8}{1,000} = \mathbf{\frac{1}{125}}$$

2. To convert a percent to a fraction, write it over a denominator of 100 and simplify.

$$420\% = \frac{420}{100} = \mathbf{\frac{21}{5}}\ (\text{improper}) = \mathbf{4\frac{1}{5}}\ (\text{mixed})$$

$$8\% = \frac{8}{100} = \mathbf{\frac{2}{25}}$$

3. To convert a fraction to a decimal, divide the numerator by the denominator.

$$\frac{9}{2} = 9 \div 2 = \mathbf{4.5}$$

It often helps to simplify the fraction BEFORE you divide:

$$\frac{3,000}{10,000} = \frac{3}{10} = \mathbf{0.3}$$

4. To convert a mixed number to a decimal, simplify the mixed number first, if needed.

$$1\,\frac{27}{4} = 1 + 6\,\frac{3}{4} = \mathbf{7.75}$$

$$12\,\frac{8}{3} = 12 + 2\,\frac{2}{3} = 14\,\frac{2}{3} = \mathbf{14.\overline{6}}$$

Note: you do not have to know the "repeating bar" notation, but you should know that 2/3 = 0.6666...

5. To convert a fraction to a percent, rewrite the fraction with a denominator of 100.

$$\frac{1,000}{10} = \frac{10,000}{100} = \mathbf{10,000\%}$$

Or convert the fraction to a decimal and shift the decimal point two places to the right.

$$\frac{25}{9} = 25 \div 9 = 2.7777\ldots = 2.\overline{7} = \mathbf{277.\overline{7}\%}$$

6. To convert a decimal to a percent, shift the decimal point two places to the right.
   80.4 = **8,040%**
   0.0007 = **0.07%**

7. $\mathbf{40\% < \dfrac{8}{18} < 0.8}$: To order from least to greatest, express all the terms in the same form.

$$\frac{8}{18} = \frac{4}{9} = 0.4444\ldots = 0.\overline{4}$$
$$0.8 = 0.8$$
$$40\% = 0.4$$
$$0.4 < 0.\overline{4} < 0.8$$

Alternately, you can use FDP logic and Benchmark Values to solve this problem: $\dfrac{8}{18}$ is $\dfrac{1}{18}$ less than $\dfrac{1}{2}$.

40% is 10% (or $\dfrac{1}{10}$) less than $\dfrac{1}{2}$. Since $\dfrac{8}{18}$ is a smaller piece away from $\dfrac{1}{2}$, it is closer to $\dfrac{1}{2}$ and

therefore larger than 40%. 0.8 is clearly greater than $\dfrac{1}{2}$. Therefore, $40\% < \dfrac{8}{18} < 0.8$.

8. $\mathbf{1.19 < 131.44\% < \dfrac{120}{84}}$: To order from least to greatest, express all the terms in the same form.

$$1.19 = 1.19$$
$$\frac{120}{84} \approx 1.4286$$
$$131.44\% = 1.3144$$
$$1.19 < 1.3144 < 1.4286$$

9. $\mathbf{2.401 < 2\dfrac{4}{7} < 2400\%}$: To order from least to greatest, express all the terms in the same form.

$$2\frac{4}{7} \approx 2.57$$
$$2400\% = 24$$
$$2.401 = 2.401$$

Alternately, you can use FDP logic and Benchmark Values to solve this problem: 2400% is 24, which is

clearly the largest value. Then, use Benchmark Values to compare $2\dfrac{4}{7}$ and 2.401. Since the whole number

portion, 2, is the same, just compare the fraction parts. $\dfrac{4}{7}$ is greater than $\dfrac{1}{2}$. 0.401 is less than $\dfrac{1}{2}$.

Therefore, $2\dfrac{4}{7}$ must be greater than 2.401. So, $2.401 < 2\dfrac{4}{7} < 2400\%$.

10. $\mathbf{3.10\% < 2.9 < \dfrac{50}{17}}$: To order from least to greatest, express all the terms in the same form.

(Note that, since x^2 is a positive term common to all the terms you are comparing, you can ignore its
presence completely. If the common term were negative, then the order would be reversed.)

$\dfrac{50}{17} = 2\dfrac{16}{17} \approx 2.94$ (You can find the first few digits of the decimal by long division.)

$2.9 = 2.9$
$3.10\% = 0.0310$
$0.0310 < 2.9 < 2.94$

Alternately, you can use FDP logic and Benchmark Values to solve this problem: 3.10% is 0.0310, which is clearly the smallest value. Then, compare 2.9 and $2\dfrac{16}{17}$ to see which one is closer to 3. 2.9 is $\dfrac{1}{10}$ away from 3. $2\dfrac{16}{17}$ is $\dfrac{1}{17}$ away from 3. Since $\dfrac{1}{17}$ is smaller than $\dfrac{1}{10}$, $2\dfrac{16}{17}$ is closest to 3; therefore, it is larger. So, $3.10\% < 2.9 < \dfrac{50}{17}$.

11. $\dfrac{500}{199} < 2.9002003 < 248,000\%$: To order from least to greatest, express all the terms in the same form.

$\dfrac{500}{199} \approx 2.51$ (You can find the first few digits of the decimal by long division.)

$248,000\% = 2,480$
$2.9002003 = 2.9002003$

Alternately, you can use FDP logic and Benchmark Values to solve this problem: 248,000% = 2,480, which is clearly the largest value. $\dfrac{500}{199}$ is approximately $\dfrac{500}{200}$, or $\dfrac{5}{2}$, which is 2.5. This is clearly less than 2.9002003. Therefore, $\dfrac{500}{199} < 2.9002003 < 248,000\%$.

12. **120:** This is a percent vs. decimal conversion problem. If you simply recognize that $62.5\% = 0.625 = \dfrac{5}{8}$, this problem will be a lot easier: $\dfrac{5}{8} \times 192 = \dfrac{5}{1} \times 24 = 120$. Multiplying 0.625×240 will take much longer to complete.

13. **1,250:** This is a percent vs. decimal conversion problem. If you simply recognize that $16\% = 0.16 = \dfrac{16}{100} = \dfrac{4}{25}$, this problem will be a lot easier: $\dfrac{4}{25}x = 200$, so $x = 200 \times \dfrac{25}{4} = 50 \times 25 = 1,250$. Dividing out $200 \div 0.16$ will probably take longer to complete.

14. $\dfrac{XY}{100}$: We can use decimal equivalents. X percent is $\dfrac{X}{100}$, and we simply need to multiply by Y.

Alternatively we can set up a table and solve for the unknown (in this case, we will call it Z):

PART	Z	X	$100Z = XY$
WHOLE	Y	100	$Z = \dfrac{XY}{100}$

15. $\dfrac{100X}{Y}$: We can use decimal equivalents. X equals some unknown percent of Y (call it Z percent), so

$X = \dfrac{Z}{100} \times Y$, and we simply solve for Z: $\dfrac{100X}{Y} = Z$.

Alternatively we can set up a table and solve for the unknown Z:

PART	X	Z	$100X = ZY$
WHOLE	Y	100	$Z = \dfrac{100X}{Y}$

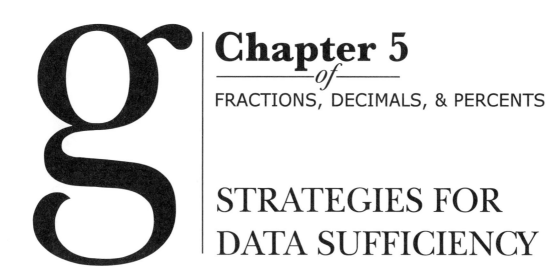

Chapter 5
of
FRACTIONS, DECIMALS, & PERCENTS

STRATEGIES FOR
DATA SUFFICIENCY

In This Chapter . . .

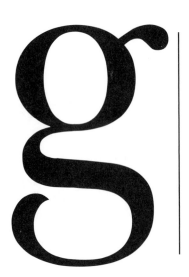

- Rephrasing: One Equation, One Variable

- Sample Rephrasings for Challenging Problems

Rephrasing: One Equation, One Variable

Data sufficiency problems that deal with FDPs usually present various parts and wholes. Keeping track of them can be difficult. Therefore, one strategy to help you solve these problems is to REPHRASE questions and statements into equations in order to keep track of what you know and what you need to know. Your ultimate goal in writing equations is to combine them in such a way that you are left with a single equation with only one variable. The variable in the equation should represent the quantity you are asked to find in the original question.

> If a brokerage firm charged a commission of 2% of the total dollar amount of a certain trade, what was the total dollar amount of that trade?
>
> (1) The dollar amount of the trade minus the brokerage firm's commission was $88,000.
> (2) The brokerage firm's commission decreased the profit earned on the trade by 20%.

(A) Statement (1) ALONE is sufficient, but statement (2) alone is not sufficient.
(B) Statement (2) ALONE is sufficient, but statement (1) alone is not sufficient.
(C) BOTH statements TOGETHER are sufficient, but NEITHER statement ALONE is sufficient.
(D) EACH statement ALONE is sufficient.
(E) Statements (1) and (2) together are NOT sufficient.

First, assign a variable to represent the unknown for which you are trying to solve:

> Let d = the total dollar amount of the trade

Then, express the information given in the question, identifying any other variables you need:

> Let c = the brokerage firm's commission
>
> $c = 0.02d$

Test each statement, writing equations to represent the information. If the information in the statement can be combined with the information in the question to yield a single equation with the single variable d, the statement is sufficient:

Statement (1): $d - c = 88,000$

> Substitute the value for c given in the question.
>
> $d - (0.02d) = 88,000$

This is a single equation with a single variable so it is sufficient to solve for d and answer the question.

Try to rephrase the part–whole relationship given in the question by writing an equation.

Statement (2) introduces a new variable into the picture: profit.

Let p = the profit before the commission

$$p - c = 0.80p$$

Since we do not know p, the amount of profit from the trade before the commission, we cannot solve for c, the brokerage firm's commission.

Since we cannot find c, we are unable to determine d, the total dollar amount of the trade. Thus, statement (2) is NOT sufficient.

The answer to this data sufficiency problem is (A): Statement (1) ALONE is sufficient, but statement (2) alone is not sufficient.

Beware of statements that introduce too many variables. These are usually not sufficient to answer the question.

Rephrasing: Challenge Short Set

In Chapters 6 and 8, you will find lists of Fractions, Decimals, and Percent problems that have appeared on past official GMAT exams. These lists refer to problems from three books published by the Graduate Management Admission Council® (the organization that develops the official GMAT exam):

The Official Guide for GMAT Review, 12th Edition
The Official Guide for GMAT Quantitative Review
The Official Guide for GMAT Quantitative Review, 2nd Edition

<u>Note</u>: The two editions of the Quant Review book largely overlap. Use one OR the other. The questions contained in these three books are the property of The Graduate Management Admission Council, which is not affiliated in any way with Manhattan GMAT.

As you work through the Data Sufficiency problems listed at the end of Part I and Part II, be sure to focus on *rephrasing*. If possible, try to *rephrase* each question into its simplest form *before* looking at the two statements. In order to rephrase, focus on figuring out the specific information that is absolutely necessary to answer the question. After rephrasing the question, you should also try to *rephrase* each of the two statements, if possible. Rephrase each statement by simplifying the given information into its most basic form.

In order to help you practice rephrasing, we have taken a set of generally difficult Data Sufficiency problems on *The Official Guide* problem list (these are the problem numbers listed in the "Challenge Short Set" on page 115) and have provided you with our own sample rephrasings for each question and statement. In order to evaluate how effectively you are using the rephrasing strategy, you can compare your rephrased questions and statements to our own rephrasings that appear below. Questions and statements that are significantly rephrased appear in **bold**.

Rephrasings from *The Official Guide For GMAT Review, 12th Edition*

The questions and statements that appear below are only our *rephrasings*. The original questions and statements can be found by referencing the problem numbers below in the Data Sufficiency section of *The Official Guide for GMAT Review, 12th edition* (pages 272–288).

D25.   What is the units digit of *n*? (Possibilities = 3, 4, 5, 6, 7, 8, or 9)

  (1) **The units digit of *n* is 5 or 6.**
  (2) **The units digit of *n* is 4, 5, 6, or 9.**

27.   Let V_{after} = the volume of oil present after the 200 gallons were removed
  Let T = the total capacity of the tank

$$V_{after} = \frac{3}{7}T$$

What is T? OR
What is V_{after}?

  (1) $V_{after} + 200 = \frac{1}{2}T$

  $$\frac{3}{7}T + 200 = \frac{1}{2}T$$

  (2) $V_{after} = T - 1{,}600$

  $$\frac{3}{7}T = T - 1{,}600$$

52. $$\frac{y-x}{x} = \frac{?}{100}$$

$$\frac{y-x}{x} = ?$$

$$\frac{y-x}{x} = \frac{y}{x} - \frac{x}{x} = \frac{y}{x} - 1 = ?$$

What is $\frac{y}{x}$?

  (1) $y - x = 20$

  (2) $\frac{y}{x} = \frac{5}{4}$

61.   Let d = the number of guests served a double scoop
  Let s = the number of guests served a single scoop

What is the value of *d*?

$\qquad$ (1) $0.6(d + s) = d$

$\qquad$ (2) $2d + s = 120$

79. $\qquad p_1\left(1 + \dfrac{t_1}{100}\right) > p_2\left(1 + \dfrac{t_2}{100}\right)?$

$\qquad p_1 + \dfrac{p_1 t_1}{100} > p_2 + \dfrac{p_2 t_2}{100}?$

$\qquad$ (1) $t_1 > t_2$

$\qquad$ (2) $p_1 t_1 > p_2 t_2$

88. $\qquad$ Let M = mortgage payments
$\qquad$ Let R = real estate taxes
$\qquad$ Let H = home insurance

$\qquad M + R + H = 12{,}000$
$\qquad$ What is R? OR
$\qquad$ **What is $M + H$?**

$\qquad$ (1) $R + H = \dfrac{1}{3}M$

$\qquad$ (2) $R = 0.20(M + H)$

$\qquad\qquad 5R = M + H$

$\qquad\qquad R + 5R = 12{,}000$

$\qquad\qquad$ **$6R = 12{,}000$**

120. $\qquad$ Let R = rent collected in 1997

$\qquad \left(1 - \dfrac{y}{100}\right)\left(1 + \dfrac{x}{100}\right) R > R?$

$\qquad \left(1 - \dfrac{y}{100}\right)\left(1 + \dfrac{x}{100}\right) > 1?$

$\qquad 1 + \dfrac{x}{100} - \dfrac{y}{100} - \dfrac{xy}{10{,}000} > 1?$

$\qquad \dfrac{x - y}{100} > \dfrac{xy}{10{,}000}?$

$\qquad$ **$x - y > \dfrac{xy}{100}?$**

$\qquad$ (1) $x > y$

$\qquad$ (2) $\dfrac{xy}{100} < x - y$

142.   Little rephrasing of the question is possible until you create a framework using the statements.

(1)

	Commission Rate (%) ×	Sales ($) =	Commission ($)
First half of 1988			?
Second half of 1988			
Total for 1988	5%		

(2)

	Commission Rate (%) ×	Sales ($) =	Commission ($)
First half of 1988		x	?
Second half of 1988		$x + 60,000$	
Total for 1988		$2x + 60,000$	

143.   Let x = the original price of stock X
Let y = the original price of stock Y

What is the value of $\dfrac{0.9y}{x}$?

What is the value of $\dfrac{y}{x}$?

   (1) $1.1x = y$

$$\dfrac{y}{x} = 1.1$$

   (2) $0.1x = \left(\dfrac{10}{11}\right)(0.1y)$

$$\dfrac{y}{x} = \dfrac{11}{10}$$

151.   What is k? OR
What is n?

   (1) $k = 51,000$
     $n = 4$

   (2) $k = \sqrt{2.601 \times 10^9}$

167.   What is the tens digit of n?

   (1) The tens digit of n is 6

   (2) **The tens digit of n is 6 or 7**

ManhattanGMAT*Prep
the new standard

Rephrasings from *The Official Guide for GMAT Quantitative Review*, 2nd Edition

The questions and statements that appear below are only our *rephrasings*. The original questions and statements can be found by referencing the problem numbers below in the Data Sufficiency section of *The Official Guide for GMAT Quantitative Review, 2nd Edition* (pages 152–163). First Edition numbers are included in parentheses. Problems unique to one edition are so indicated.

5.
(5.)   Let x = the percent discount at which the TV was bought
        Let y = the percent mark-up at which the TV was sold
        Let z = the original (list) price

Purchase Price = $z \times \dfrac{(100 - x)}{100}$ and Sale Price = $z \times \dfrac{(100 - y)}{100}$

What is the value of z?

(1) $x = 15$

(2) $y = x - 5$

(22. 1st Edition only)
        Let s = money awarded to the spouse
        Let a = money awarded to the oldest child
        Let b = money awarded to the middle child
        Let c = money awarded to the youngest child

$s + a + b + c = 200,000$
$c = 200,000 - (a + b + s)$

What is the value of c?

(1) **$s = 100,000$**
    $a = 25,000$

(2) **$b = c$**
    $a = c - 12,500$
    $s = c + 62,500$

49.   The easiest way to solve this problem is to test numbers, making sure to test both integer and
(48.)   decimal values for r and s.

50.   Let n = the number of shares
(49.)

What is the value of $\dfrac{12,000}{n}$?

What is the value of n?

(1) $n(\dfrac{12{,}000}{n} + 1) = \$12{,}300$

$$12{,}000 + n = \$12{,}300$$
$$\boldsymbol{n = 300}$$

(2) $n(\dfrac{12{,}000}{n} - 2) = 0.95(\$12{,}300)$

$$12{,}000 - 2n = 11{,}400$$
$$2n = 600$$
$$\boldsymbol{n = 300}$$

75.   Let r = the number of games remaining for Team A
(72.)   Let t = total number of games played by Team $A = 20 + r$
         Let w = games won by Team $A = 10 + r$

What is the value of w?
Better: What is the value of r?

(1) $t = 25$
(2) $\dfrac{w}{t} = \dfrac{10 + r}{20 + r} = 0.60$

$$10 + r = 12 + 0.6r$$
$$0.4r = 2$$
$$\boldsymbol{r = 5}$$

96. 2nd Edition only

     Is $-1 < x \leq 0$?   In other words, is $-1 < x$ AND is $x \leq 0$?

     (1) No rephrasing necessary
     (2) $0 < x + 0.5 \leq 1$
         $\boldsymbol{-0.5 < x \leq 0.5}$

119.   The easiest way to solve this problem is to test numbers.
(113.)

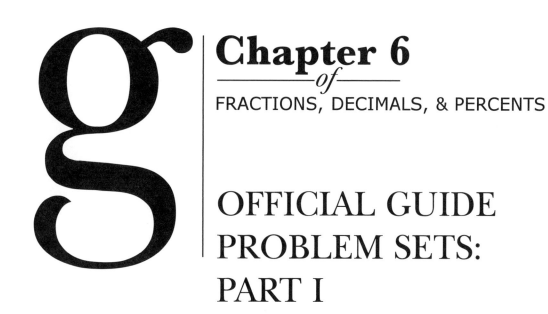

Chapter 6
of
FRACTIONS, DECIMALS, & PERCENTS

OFFICIAL GUIDE
PROBLEM SETS:
PART I

In This Chapter . . .

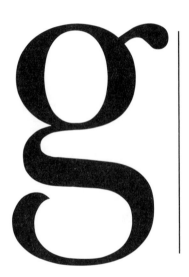

- Fractions, Decimals, & Percents Problem Solving List from *The Official Guides:* PART I
- Fractions, Decimals, & Percents Data Sufficiency List from *The Official Guides:* PART I

Practicing with REAL GMAT Problems

Now that you have completed Part I of FRACTIONS, DECIMALS, & PERCENTS, it is time to test your skills on problems that have actually appeared on real GMAT exams over the past several years.

The problem sets that follow are composed of questions from three books published by the Graduate Management Admission Council® (the organization that develops the official GMAT exam):

The Official Guide for GMAT Review, 12th Edition
The Official Guide for GMAT Quantitative Review
The Official Guide for GMAT Quantitative Review, 2nd Edition
Note: The two editions of the Quant Review book largely overlap. Use one OR the other.

These books contain quantitative questions that have appeared on past official GMAT exams. (The questions contained therein are the property of The Graduate Management Admission Council, which is not affiliated in any way with Manhattan GMAT.)

Although the questions in the Official Guides have been "retired" (they will not appear on future official GMAT exams), they are great practice questions.

In order to help you practice effectively, we have categorized every problem in The Official Guides by topic and subtopic. On the following pages, you will find two categorized lists:

(1) **Problem Solving:** Lists EASIER Problem Solving Fraction, Decimal, and Percent questions contained in *The Official Guides* and categorizes them by subtopic.

(2) **Data Sufficiency:** Lists EASIER Data Sufficiency Fraction, Decimal, and Percent questions contained in *The Official Guides* and categorizes them by subtopic.

The remaining *Official Guide* problems are listed at the end of Part II of this book. **Do not forget about the Part II list!**

Each book in Manhattan GMAT's 8–book strategy series contains its own *Official Guide* lists that pertain to the specific topic of that particular book. If you complete all the practice problems contained on the *Official Guide* lists in each of the 8 Manhattan GMAT strategy books, you will have completed every single question published in *The Official Guides*.

Problem Solving: Part I

from *The Official Guide for GMAT Review, 12th Edition* (pages 20–23 & 152–185), *The Official Guide for GMAT Quantitative Review* (pages 62–85), and *The Official Guide for GMAT Quantitative Review, 2nd Edition* (pages 62–86).

Note: The two editions of the Quant Review book largely overlap. Use one OR the other.

Solve each of the following problems in a notebook, making sure to demonstrate how you arrived at each answer by showing all of your work and computations. If you get stuck on a problem, look back at the FDP strategies and content in this guide to assist you.

Note: Problem numbers preceded by "D" refer to questions in the Diagnostic Test chapter of *The Official Guide for GMAT Review, 12th edition* (pages 20–23).

<u>GENERAL SET – FRACTIONS, DECIMALS, & PERCENTS</u>

Fractions
> *12th Edition*: 24, 37, 43, 45, 74, 95, 138, 175, 176, D8
> *Quantitative Review*: 5, 11, 37, 39, 44, 46, 48, 51, 57, 61, 73, 79, 88, 108, 112, 134, 135
> OR *2nd Edition*: 8, 14, 39, 42, 46, 48, 50, 53, 59, 60, 61, 69, 88, 134

Digits and Decimals
> *12th Edition*: 15, 28, 79, 114, 129, 133, 143, 182, D1, D11
> *Quantitative Review*: 2, 4, 41, 65, 66, 93
> OR *2nd Edition*: 4, 6, 65, 93

Percents
> *12th Edition*: 8, 13, 19, 47, 61, 78, 123, 128, 131, 139, D21
> *Quantitative Review*: 8, 10, 13, 24, 33, 47, 74, 95, 101, 114, 120
> OR *2nd Edition*: 10, 12, 26, 35, 49, 73, 95, 101, 114, 120

Successive Percents and Percent Change
> *12th Edition*: 17, 60, 64, 92, 94, 109, 111, 115, D12
> *Quantitative Review*: 6, 36, 40, 67, 89
> OR *2nd Edition*: 9, 38, 43, 66, 89

FDPs
> *12th Edition*: 10, 56
> *Quantitative Review*: 25, 27, 43, 56
> OR *2nd Edition*: 27, 29, 45, 58

Remember, there are more Official Guide problems listed at the end of Part II.

Data Sufficiency: Part I

from *The Official Guide for GMAT Review, 12th Edition* (pages 24–26 & 272–288), *The Official Guide for GMAT Quantitative Review* (pages 149–157), and *The Official Guide for GMAT Quantitative Review, 2nd Edition* (pages 152–163).

<u>Note</u>: The two editions of the Quant Review book largely overlap. Use one OR the other.

Solve each of the following problems in a notebook, making sure to demonstrate how you arrived at each answer by showing all of your work and computations. If you get stuck on a problem, look back at the FDP strategies and content contained in this guide to assist you.

Practice REPHRASING both the questions and the statements by using variables and constructing equations. The majority of data sufficiency problems can be rephrased; however, if you have difficulty rephrasing a problem, try testing numbers to solve it. It is especially important that you familiarize yourself with the directions for data sufficiency problems, and that you memorize the 5 fixed answer choices that accompany all data sufficiency problems.

<u>Note</u>: Problem numbers preceded by "D" refer to questions in the Diagnostic Test chapter of *The Official Guide for GMAT Review, 12th edition* (pages 24–26).

GENERAL SET – FRACTIONS, DECIMALS, & PERCENTS

Fractions
> *12th Edition*: 9, 27, 59
> *Quantitative Review*: 2, 22 OR *2nd Edition*: 2, 48

Digits and Decimals
> *12th Edition*: 31, 41, 64, 100
> *Quantitative Review*: 30, 44, 48 OR *2nd Edition*: 21, 30, 44, 49

Percents
> *12th Edition*: 2, 7, 33, 37, 48, 61, 63, 77, 79, D40
> *Quantitative Review*: 5, 36, 49, 52, 72, 89
> OR *2nd Edition*: 5, 36, 50, 53, 75, 93

Successive Percents and Percent Change
> *12th Edition*: 55
> *Quantitative Review*: 1

FDPs
> *12th Edition*: 43, 46, 52, 85

Remember, there are more Official Guide problems listed at the end of Part II.

PART II: ADVANCED

This part of the book covers various advanced topics within *Fractions, Decimals, & Percents*. This advanced material may not be necessary for all students. Attempt Part II only if you have completed Part I and are comfortable with its content.

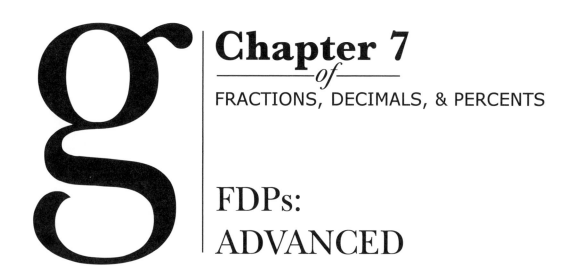

Chapter 7
of
FRACTIONS, DECIMALS, & PERCENTS

FDPs:
ADVANCED

In This Chapter . . .

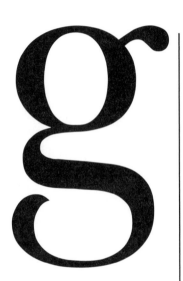

FDPs: ADVANCED

This chapter outlines miscellaneous advanced topics within the area of *Fractions, Decimals, & Percents*.

Repeating Decimals

Dividing an integer by another integer yields a decimal that either terminates (see below) or that never ends and repeats itself.

$2 \div 9 = ?$

$$\begin{array}{r} 0.222... \\ 9\overline{)2.000} \\ \underline{1.8} \\ 20 \\ \underline{18} \\ 20 \end{array}$$

$2 \div 9 = 0.2222... = 0.\overline{2}$

The bar above the 2 indicates that the digit 2 repeats forever. You will not have to use the bar on the GMAT; it is simply a convenient shorthand.

Generally, you should just do long division to determine the repeating cycle. However, it is worth noting the following patterns, which have appeared in published GMAT questions.

$4 \div 9 = 0.4444... = 0.\overline{4}$ $23 \div 99 = 0.2323... = 0.\overline{23}$

$\dfrac{1}{11} = \dfrac{9}{99} = 0.0909... = 0.\overline{09}$ $\dfrac{3}{11} = \dfrac{27}{99} = 0.2727... = 0.\overline{27}$

If the denominator is 9, 99, 999 or another number equal to a power of 10 minus 1, then the numerator gives you the repeating digits (perhaps with leading zeroes). Again, you can always find the decimal pattern by simple long division.

Terminating Decimals

Some numbers, like $\sqrt{2}$ and π, have decimals that never end and <u>never</u> repeat themselves. The GMAT will only ask you for approximations for these decimals (e.g., $\sqrt{2} \approx 1.4$). Occasionally, though, the GMAT asks you about properties of "terminating" decimals: that is, decimals that end. You can tack on zeroes, of course, but they do not matter. Here are some examples of terminating decimals: 0.2   0.47   0.375

Terminating decimals can all be written as a ratio of integers (which might be reducible):

$$\dfrac{\text{Some integer}}{\text{Some power of ten}}$$

$$0.2 = \dfrac{2}{10} = \dfrac{1}{5} \qquad 0.47 = \dfrac{47}{100} \qquad 0.375 = \dfrac{375}{1000} = \dfrac{3}{8}$$

Positive powers of ten are composed of only 2's and 5's as prime factors. This means that when you reduce this fraction, you only have prime factors of 2's and/or 5's in the denominator. Every terminating decimal shares this characteristic. If, after being fully reduced, the denominator has any prime factors besides 2 or 5, then its decimal will not terminate. If the denominator only has factors of 2 and/or 5, then the decimal will terminate.

> When you express terminating decimals as fractions in lowest terms, they only have 2's and/or 5's as prime factors in their denominators.

Unknown Digit Problems

Occasionally, the GMAT asks tough problems involving unknown digits. These problems look like "brainteasers"; it seems it could take all day to test the possible digits.

However, like all other GMAT problems, these digit "brainteasers" must be solvable under time constraints. As a result, you always have ways of reducing the number of possibilities.

Principles: (1) Look at the answer choices first, to limit your search.
                 (2) Use other given constraints to rule out additional possibilities.
                 (3) Focus on the units digit in the product or sum.
                      This units digit is affected by the fewest other digits.
                 (4) Test the remaining answer choices.

Example:

$$
\begin{array}{r}
AB \\
\times\ CA \\
\hline
DEBC
\end{array}
$$

In the multiplication above, each letter stands for a different non–zero digit, with $A \times B < 10$. What is the two–digit number AB?

(A) 23 (B) 24 (C) 25 (D) 32 (E) 42

It is often helpful to look at the answer choices. Here, we see that the possible digits for A and B are 2, 3, 4, and 5.

Next, apply the given constraint that $A \times B < 10$. This rules out answer choice (C), 25, since $2 \times 5 = 10$.

Now, test the remaining answer choices. Notice that $A \times B = C$, the units digit of the product. Therefore, you can find all the needed digits and complete each multiplication.

Compare each result to the template. The two positions of the B digit must match.

$$
\begin{array}{r}
23 \\
\times\ 62 \\
\hline
1,426
\end{array}
\qquad\qquad
\begin{array}{r}
24 \\
\times\ 82 \\
\hline
1,968
\end{array}
$$

The B's do not match   The B's do not match

$$
\begin{array}{r}
32 \\
\times\ 63 \\
\hline
2,016
\end{array}
\qquad\qquad
\begin{array}{r}
42 \\
\times\ 84 \\
\hline
3,528
\end{array}
$$

The B's do not match   The B's match   Answer is **(E)**.

Note that you could have used the constraints to derive the possible digits (2, 3, and 4) without using the answer choices. However, for these problems, you should take advantage of the answer choices to restrict your search quickly.

Formulas That Act on Decimals

Occasionally, you might encounter a formula or special symbol that acts on decimals. Follow the formula's instructions <u>precisely</u>.

Let us define symbol [x] to represent the largest integer less than or equal to x.

> What is [5.1]?

According to the definition we are given, [5.1] is the largest integer less than or equal to 5.1. That integer is 5. So [5.1] = 5.

> What is [0.8]?

According to the definition again, [0.8] is the largest integer less than or equal to 0.8. That integer is 0. So [0.8] = 0. Notice that the result is NOT 1. This particular definition does not round the number. Rather, the operation *seems* to be truncation—simply cutting off the decimal. However, we must be careful with negatives.

> What is [−2.3]?

Once again, [−2.3] is the largest integer less than or equal to −2.3. Remember that "less than" on a number line means "to the left of." A "smaller" negative number is further away from zero than a "bigger" negative number. So the largest integer less than −2.3 is −3, and [−2.3] = −3. Notice that the result is NOT −2; this bracket operation is NOT truncation.

Be sure to follow the instructions exactly whenever you are given a special symbol or formula involving decimals. It is easy to jump to conclusions about how an operation works: for instance, finding the largest integer less than x is NOT the same as rounding x or truncating x in all cases. Also, do not confuse this particular set of brackets [x] with parentheses (x) or absolute value signs |x|.

When you work with formulas that act on decimals, avoid shortcuts and follow directions!

Fractions and Exponents & Roots

On many GMAT problems, you need to know what happens to a fraction when you raise it to a power. The result depends on the size and sign of the fraction, as well as on the power:

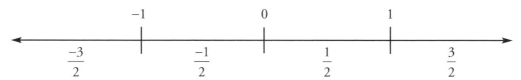

EVEN EXPONENTS (such as 2):

$$\left(\frac{-3}{2}\right)^2 = \frac{9}{4} \qquad \left(\frac{-1}{2}\right)^2 = \frac{1}{4} \qquad \left(\frac{1}{2}\right)^2 = \frac{1}{4} \qquad \left(\frac{3}{2}\right)^2 = \frac{9}{4}$$

$$\frac{-3}{2} < \frac{9}{4} \qquad\qquad \frac{-1}{2} < \frac{1}{4} \qquad\qquad \frac{1}{2} > \frac{1}{4} \qquad\qquad \frac{3}{2} < \frac{9}{4}$$

result is bigger   result is bigger   result is SMALLER   result is bigger

ODD EXPONENTS (such as 3):

$$\left(\frac{-3}{2}\right)^3 = \frac{-27}{8} \qquad \left(\frac{-1}{2}\right)^3 = \frac{-1}{8} \qquad \left(\frac{1}{2}\right)^3 = \frac{1}{8} \qquad \left(\frac{3}{2}\right)^3 = \frac{27}{8}$$

$$\frac{-3}{2} > \frac{-27}{8} \qquad \frac{-1}{2} < \frac{-1}{8} \qquad \frac{1}{2} > \frac{1}{8} \qquad \frac{3}{2} < \frac{27}{8}$$

result is SMALLER   result is bigger   result is SMALLER   result is bigger

As you can see, the effect of raising a fraction to a power varies depending upon the fraction's value, sign, and the exponent.

Be ready to re-generate these outcomes with test numbers such as $\frac{1}{2}$.

To raise a fraction to a negative power, simply raise the reciprocal to the equivalent positive power.

$$\left(\frac{3}{7}\right)^{-2} = \left(\frac{7}{3}\right)^2 = \frac{7^2}{3^2} = \frac{49}{9} \qquad\qquad \left(\frac{x}{y}\right)^{-w} = \left(\frac{y}{x}\right)^w = \frac{y^w}{x^w}$$

Finally, remember that taking a root of a number is the same thing as raising that number to a fractional power.

$$\sqrt{81} = (81)^{1/2} = 9 \qquad\qquad \sqrt[4]{x^3} = \left(x^3\right)^{1/4} = x^{3/4}$$

As a particular example, note that taking the square root of a proper fraction raises its value toward 1.

For more review of exponents and roots, see the *Number Properties* Strategy Guide.

> When you raise a fraction to a power, pay attention to both the sign and the size (relative to +1 or −1) of the fraction.

Percents and Weighted Averages

A mixture chart can be used to solve weighted average problems that involve percents.

> Kris–P cereal is 10% sugar by weight, whereas healthier but less delicious Bran–O cereal is 2% sugar by weight. To make a delicious *and* healthy mixture that is 4% sugar, what should be the ratio of Kris–P cereal to Bran–O cereal, by weight?

First, set up a mixture chart. This time, instead of Original/Change/New, put the cereal brands and Total across the top. We will also put the parts of each cereal in the rows.

Pounds (lbs)	Kris–P	Bran–O	Total
Sugar			
Other stuff			
Total Cereal			

the new standard

We are not given any actual weights in this problem, nor are we asked for any such weights. As a result, we can pick one Smart Number. Let us pick the total amount of Kris–P: 100 pounds (lbs). Now we can compute how much sugar is in that Kris–P: $(0.10)(100) = 10$ lbs. Do not bother computing the weight of the "other stuff"; it rarely matters.

Pounds (lbs)	Kris–P	Bran–O	Total
Sugar	10		
Other stuff			
Total Cereal	100		

Now set the total amount of Bran–O as x lb (we cannot pick another Smart Number). Since Bran–O is only 2% sugar, the mass of sugar in the Bran–O will be $(0.02)x$ lb. We can now add up the bottom row: the total amount of all cereals is $100 + x$ lb. Since the total mixture is 4% sugar, the weight of sugar in the mixture is $(0.04)(100 + x)$ lb.

Pounds (lbs)	Kris–P	Bran–O	Total
Sugar	10	$(0.02)x$	$(0.04)(100 + x)$
Other stuff			
Total Cereal	100	x	$100 + x$

Finally, we can write an equation summing the top row (the amounts of sugar):

$$10 + (0.02)x = (0.04)(100 + x) \qquad 6 = (0.02)x$$
$$10 + (0.02)x = 4 + (0.04)x \qquad 300 = x$$

The ratio of Kris–P to Bran–O is 100 : 300 or 1 : 3.

This result should make sense: to make a 4% mixture out of 10% and 2% cereals, you need much more of the 2%. In fact, 4% is the average of 10% and 2%, weighted 1 to 3.

Percent Change and Weighted Averages

Weighted averages can also show up in "percent change" problems.

> A company sells only pens and pencils. The revenue from pen sales in 2007 was up 5% from 2006, but the revenue from pencil sales declined 13% over the same period. If overall revenue was down 1% from 2006 to 2007, what was the ratio of pencil revenues to pen revenues in 2006?

First, set up a chart. We will use the Original/Change/New framework, but we will write 2006 and 2007 in the column headers. We will write Pen and Pencil Revenue in the row headers.

Dollars ($)	2006	Change	2007
Pen Revenue			
Pencil Revenue			
Total Revenue			

Make sure that you set up your mixture chart both to sum across and to sum down, making a Total column and row.

As in the previous problem, we are not given any actual amounts (in this case, dollar revenue), nor are we asked for any such revenue in dollar terms. Rather, we are asked for a ratio of revenue. As a result, we can pick one Smart Number. Let us pick $100 for the 2006 Pen Revenue. Since that revenue went up 5%, the change is +$5, and the 2007 Pen Revenue is $105. Remember, all amounts are in some monetary unit (say, dollars).

Dollars ($)	2006	Change	2007
Pen Revenue	100	+5	105
Pencil Revenue			
Total Revenue			

Now set the 2006 Pencil Revenue equal to x. Remember, you cannot pick another Smart Number, since you do not know what the ratio of 2006 revenue will be. Since the Pencil Revenue went down 13%, the change in dollar terms is $-0.13x$, and the 2007 Pencil Revenue is $0.87x$ dollars.

You can also write the 2006 Total Revenue as the sum of that column. Since the Total Revenue went down 1%, the change (again, in dollar terms) is $-0.01(100 + x)$, and the 2007 Total Revenue is $0.99(100 + x)$

Dollars ($)	2006	Change	2007
Pen Revenue	100	+5	105
Pencil Revenue	x	$-0.13x$	$0.87x$
Total Revenue	$100 + x$	$-0.01(100 + x)$	$0.99(100 + x)$

Finally, we can write an equation summing the 2007 column:

$$105 + 0.87x = 0.99(100 + x)$$
$$105 + 0.87x = 99 + 0.99x$$
$$6 = 0.12x$$
$$600 = 12x$$
$$50 = x$$

Since the 2006 Pen Revenue is $100, the ratio of Pencil Revenue to Pen Revenue in 2006 is 50 : 100, or 1 : 2.

Be sure to answer the question exactly as given! The problem could easily ask for the ratio of Pen Revenue to Pencil Revenue in 2007, or for the ratio of either part to the total.

Again, this result should make sense. A 5% increase in Pen Revenue and a 13% decline in Pencil Revenue only average to a 1% decline overall if there is proportionally more Pen Revenue to start with. If the 2006 revenue of pens and pencils were equal, then the average change would just be a straight average (arithmetic mean):

$$\frac{+5\% + (-13\%)}{2} = \frac{-8\%}{2} = -4\%$$

*Manhattan*GMAT*Prep
the new standard

Use an Original/Change/New chart to compute the weighted average of percent changes.

As it stands, however, the overall percent change is a *weighted* average of the two percent changes. The weights are the 2006 (original) revenues:

$$\frac{(+5\%)(100)+(-13\%)(50)}{100+50}=\frac{+5-6.5}{150}=\frac{-1.5}{150}=-1\%$$

You can use a similar formula to solve for the $50 and thus the revenue ratio. The algebraic steps are the same as they are with the chart.

$$\frac{(+5\%)(100)+(-13\%)(x)}{100+x}=-1\%$$

In fact, to solve this equation for *x*, you can simply leave the percents as percents, rather than change them to decimals.

Last, do not forget that on any real GMAT problem, you can plug in answer choices. You will always be given the correct ratio in one of the answer choices. Simply pick an answer choice (say, a ratio of 1 : 3) and invent revenues based on that ratio (say, $100 : $300). Then work forward from there, finding the changes in revenue per product and overall revenue. Compare your results to the overall change given. Repeat as necessary. This method can be computationally intensive, but it will produce the correct answer eventually in many situations.

For more on Weighted Averages, see the *Word Translations* Strategy Guide.

> If you use a formula to write the weighted average of percent changes directly, you can leave the percents as percents (keeping the % sign) when you solve.

Other Percent Changes

You can calculate a percent change for any value that changes—even if that value is itself a fraction, a ratio, a decimal, or a percent. Just keep the labels straight and plug into the two "percent change" equations:

Original + Change = New $\dfrac{\text{Change}}{\text{Original}}$ = Percent Change

Consider the following problem:

> In the first quarter of 2008, Harry's Hardware Store sold 300 hammers and 12,000 nails. In the second quarter of 2008, the store sold 375 hammers and 18,000 nails. By approximately what percent did the ratio of hammers sold to nails sold decrease from the first quarter to the second quarter?
>
> (A) 0.4%   (B) 2.1%   (C) 2.5%   (D) 17%   (E) 25%

The value that we care about is the ratio of hammers sold to nails sold. Thus, we should calculate this value at various points in time.

$$\text{Original}=\frac{\text{Hammers}}{\text{Nails}}=\frac{300}{12,000}=\frac{300}{12,000}=\frac{1}{40}$$

Note that if you calculate the decimal equivalent of 1/40, you get 0.025 or 2.5%. If you had to guess at this point, do not guess 2.5%! The answer choices on problems such as this one often contain values that you might calculate along the way to an answer.

$$\text{New} = \frac{\text{Hammers}}{\text{Nails}} = \frac{375}{18,000}$$

Rather than simplify this fraction, we should remember what we are looking for: the percent change from Original to New. If we now figure out the percent OF the Original that the New represents, we can easily subtract 100% from that percent to get the percent decrease. The percent OF Original comes from the ratio $\dfrac{\text{New}}{\text{Original}}$, and if we set up this fraction, we will see how to cancel factors efficiently.

You can measure the percent change of a ratio as long as you keep track of the ratio's Original value, its New value, and its absolute change.

$$\frac{\text{New}}{\text{Original}} = \frac{\dfrac{375}{18,000}}{\dfrac{300}{12,000}} = \frac{375}{18,000} \times \frac{12,000}{300} = \frac{375}{18,000} \times \frac{12,000}{300} = \frac{375}{300} \times \frac{12}{18} \frac{2}{3}$$

$$= \frac{750}{900} = \frac{15 \times 5}{15 \times 6} = \frac{5}{6} \approx 83\%$$

Now, if the New is 83% of the Original, the Change is 83% − 100% = −17% of the Original. We can drop the negative sign, since the question asks how much the ratio decreased. The correct answer is (D) 17%.

Be aware of the traps in the incorrect answer choices. The New ratio works out to approximately 0.021, or 2.1% as a percent. Moreover, if you subtract the New from the Original, you get approximately 0.004, or 0.4%. However, you must remember to divide by the Original, in order to obtain a percent change. Finally, the trap in (E) 25% is this: the numerator of the ratio grew by 25% (from 300 to 375), but the denominator of the ratio grew by 50% (from 12,000 to 18,000). You may NOT simply subtract these numbers to determine the percent change of the ratio.

Estimating Decimal Equivalents

When you are estimating the decimal equivalent of a fraction, you often have a few choices.

Estimate a decimal equivalent for $\dfrac{9}{52}$. (By long division, $\dfrac{9}{52} \approx 0.173077...$)

Choice (1): Make the denominator the nearest factor of 100 or another power of 10.

$$\frac{9}{52} \approx \frac{9}{50} = \frac{18}{100} = 0.18 > \text{real value} \quad \text{(High estimate: we lowered the denominator.)}$$

Choice (2): Change the numerator or denominator to make the fraction simplify easily.

$$\frac{9}{52} \approx \frac{9}{54} = \frac{1}{6} = 0.1\overline{6} < \text{real value} \quad \text{(Low estimate: we raised the denominator.)}$$

Try not to change both the numerator and denominator, especially in opposite directions. But in a pinch, you *can* adjust both numbers – especially if your estimation does not have to be that precise (e.g., in order to eliminate answers of a drastically different size).

$$\frac{9}{52} \approx \frac{10}{50} = \frac{1}{5} = 0.2 \gg \text{real value} \quad \text{(We raised the top } and \text{ lowered the bottom.)}$$

If you need a more precise estimate, you can average a couple of methods, or you can think about *small percent adjustments*:

Estimate $\dfrac{100{,}000}{96}$. (By the calculator, $\dfrac{100{,}000}{96} = 1{,}041.\overline{6}$)

We first adjust the denominator to 100 and perform the division:

$$\frac{100{,}000}{96} \approx \frac{100{,}000}{100} = 1{,}000 < \text{real value} \quad \text{(We raised the denominator.)}$$

Now, you can make the following **approximation**, as long as you realize it is **never exact**, and that you can only use it for small adjustments. Use with caution!

You increased the denominator from 96 to 100. That is *approximately* a 4% increase.

$$\frac{\text{Change}}{\text{Original}} = \frac{4}{96} \approx \frac{4}{100}$$

This means that you can increase the result by 4%, to make your estimate more accurate:

$$1{,}000\left(1.04\right) = 1{,}040$$

Notice how close this estimate is to the real value (1,040 is 99.84% of $1{,}041.\overline{6}$).

Problem Set (Advanced)

1. What is the units digit of $\left(\dfrac{6^6}{6^5}\right)^6$?

2. Which of the following decimals can be expressed as a fraction or ratio of integers? (Choose all that apply.)

    (A) π (B) $0.\overline{146}$ (C) 1.3984375 (D) $\sqrt{2}$

3. What is the length of the sequence of different digits in the decimal equivalent of $\dfrac{3}{7}$?

4. Which of the following fractions will terminate when expressed as a decimal? (Choose all that apply.)

    (A) $\dfrac{1}{256}$ (B) $\dfrac{27}{100}$ (C) $\dfrac{100}{27}$ (D) $\dfrac{231}{660}$ (E) $\dfrac{7}{105}$

5.

    In the multiplication above, each symbol represents a different unknown digit, and $\bullet \times \blacksquare \times \blacklozenge = 36$. What is the three digit integer $\bullet\blacksquare\blacklozenge$?

    (A) 263   (B) 236   (C) 194   (D) 491   (E) 452

Determine whether problems #6–10 are TRUE or FALSE.

6. $\left(\dfrac{-3}{4}\right)^2 > -\dfrac{3}{4}$

7. $\left(\dfrac{-3}{4}\right)^3 > -\dfrac{3}{4}$

8. $\left(\dfrac{-4}{3}\right)^3 > -\dfrac{4}{3}$

9. $\left(\dfrac{x+1}{x}\right)^{-2} > \dfrac{x+1}{x}$, where x is a positive integer.

10. $\sqrt[4]{\left(\dfrac{3}{4}\right)^3} > \dfrac{3}{4}$

11. A professional gambler has won 40% of his 25 poker games for the week so far. If, all of a sudden, his luck changes and he begins winning 80% of the time, how many more games must he play to end up winning 60% of all his games for the week?

$\mathcal{Manhattan}$GMAT*Prep

12. A feed store sells two varieties of birdseed: Brand A, which is 40% millet and 60% sun-flower, and Brand B, which is 65% millet and 35% safflower. If a customer purchases a mix of the two types of birdseed that is 50% millet, what percent of the mix is Brand A?

13. A grocery store sells two varieties of jellybean jars, and each type of jellybean jar contains only red and yellow jellybeans. If Jar B contains 20% more red jellybeans than Jar A, but 10% fewer yellow jellybeans, and Jar A contains twice as many red jellybeans as yellow jellybeans, by what percent is the number of jellybeans in Jar B larger than the number of jellybeans in Jar A?

14. Last year, all registered voters in Kumannia voted either for the Revolutionary Party or for the Status Quo Party. This year, the number of Revolutionary voters increased 10%, while the number of Status Quo voters increased 5%. No other votes were cast. If the number of total voters increased 8%, what fraction of voters voted Revolutionary this year?

15. Express the following as fractions: 0.15%   9.6%

16. Express the following as decimals: 2,000%   0.030%

17. Express the following as percents: 36.1456   1

18. Order from least to greatest: $\dfrac{\dfrac{3}{5}}{\dfrac{8}{10}}$ $\dfrac{0.00751}{0.01}$ $\dfrac{200}{3} \times 10^{-2}$

19. A credit card changed its rebate program from $2.50 rebated for every $500 spent to $3 rebated for every $800 spent. By what percent did the ratio of rebate to spending decline?

For problems #20–23, express your answer in terms of the variables given (X, Y, and possibly Z).

20. What number is X% greater than Y?

21. X is what percent greater than Y?

22. X is what percent greater than Y percent of Z?

23. Estimate the following fractions in terms of decimals, and note whether your estimate is greater than or less than the real value:

$$\dfrac{12}{37} \qquad \dfrac{14}{90} \qquad \dfrac{13}{51} \qquad \dfrac{168}{839}$$

1. **6:** First, use the rules for combining exponents to simplify the expression $\dfrac{6^6}{6^5}$. We subtract the exponents

to get $\dfrac{6^6}{6^5} = 6$. Then, raise this to the sixth power: $6^6 = 6^2 \times 6^2 \times 6^2 = 36 \times 36 \times 36$. Ignore any digits other

than the last one: $6 \times 6 \times 6 = 36 \times 6$. Again, ignore any digits other than the last one: $6 \times 6 = 36$. The last digit is 6.

2. **(B) and (C):** Recall that any fraction can be expressed as a repeating or terminating decimal, and any repeating or terminating decimal can be expressed as a fraction. (A) does not exhibit a repeating pattern in the digits of the decimal ($\pi = 3.14159...$, but the pattern does not repeat at any point), nor does (D) ($\sqrt{2} = 1.41421...$, and again, the pattern does not repeat itself). Therefore, (A) and (D) cannot be expressed as a fraction. The decimal in (B) exhibits a repeating pattern: $0.\overline{146} = 0.146146146... = \dfrac{146}{999}$. The decimal in

(C) terminates, so it can be expressed as the fraction $\dfrac{13,984,375}{10,000,000}$, which is equal to $\dfrac{179}{128}$ in fully reduced

form. Note that you <u>do not</u> need to calculate these fractions to answer the question; you only need to be able to determine *whether* the decimals can be expressed as a fraction.

3. **6:** Generally, the easiest way to find the pattern of digits in a non-terminating decimal is to simply do the long division and wait for the pattern to repeat (see long division at right). This results in a repeating pattern of $0.\overline{428571}$.

$$
\begin{array}{r}
0.4285714 \\
7\overline{)3.0000000} \\
0 \\
\hline
3.0 \\
2.8 \\
\hline
20 \\
-14 \\
\hline
60 \\
-56 \\
\hline
40 \\
-35 \\
\hline
50 \\
-49 \\
\hline
10 \\
-7 \\
\hline
30 \\
-28 \\
\hline
2
\end{array}
$$

4. **(A), (B) and (D):** Recall that in order for the decimal version of a fraction to terminate, the fraction's denominator in fully reduced form must have a prime factorization that consists of only 2's and/or 5's. The denominator in (A) is composed of only 2's ($256 = 2^8$). The denominator in (B) is composed of

only 2's and 5's ($100 = 2^2 \times 5^2$). In fully reduced form, the fraction in (D) is equal to $\dfrac{7}{20}$, and 20 is com-

posed of only 2's and 5's ($20 = 2^2 \times 5$). By contrast, the denominator in (C) has prime factors other that

2's and 5's ($27 = 3^3$), and in fully reduced form, the fraction in (E) is equal to $\dfrac{1}{15}$, and 15 has a prime

factor other than 2's and 5's ($15 = 3 \times 5$).

5. **(B):** For these types of problems, it is usually easiest to eliminate answer choices that violate some constraint in the problem, then use the remaining answer choices to see which fits the pattern. (E) can be ruled out, because $4 \times 5 \times 2 \neq 36$. Additionally, notice the units column of the multiplication: the units digit of the two numbers are the same, and that digit is the same as the units digit of the result. Which digits have this property? Only 1, 5, 6, and 0. 5 and 0 are not possible here, so ◆ = 1 or 6. That eliminates (A) and (C). Multiplying out (B) and (D), we see that $26 \times 36 = 936$, and $41 \times 91 = 3,731$. Notice that the tens digit of the result needs to match the tens digit of the 3-digit number (■), and that is only true in answer choice (B). (Also notice that the result needs to be a 3-digit number, and (D) gives a 4-digit number as the result.)

6. **TRUE:** Any negative number raised to an even power will be larger than the original number, because the result will always be positive:

$$\left(\frac{-3}{4}\right)^2 = \frac{9}{16} > -\frac{3}{4}$$

7. **TRUE:** Any proper fraction raised to a power greater than 1 will decrease. Any negative number raised to an odd power will be negative. Therefore, any negative proper fraction raised to an odd power will be a smaller negative number than the original negative fraction. Since it is a smaller negative, it is a larger number:

$$\left(\frac{-3}{4}\right)^3 = -\frac{27}{64} > -\frac{3}{4}$$

8. **FALSE:** Any improper fraction raised to a power greater than 1 will increase. Any negative number raised to an odd power will be negative. Therefore, any negative improper fraction raised to an odd power will be a larger negative number than the original negative fraction. Since it is a larger negative, it is a smaller number:

$$\left(\frac{-4}{3}\right)^3 = -\frac{64}{27} < -\frac{4}{3}$$

9. **FALSE:** Any number $\dfrac{x+1}{x}$, where x is positive, will be greater than 1. Therefore, raising that number to a negative exponent will result in a number smaller than 1: $\left(\dfrac{x+1}{x}\right)^{-2} = \left(\dfrac{x}{x+1}\right)^2 < \dfrac{x+1}{x}$ whenever x is a positive number.

10. **TRUE:** $\dfrac{3}{4}$ is a proper fraction. Any positive proper fraction raised to a power greater than 1 will result in a number smaller than the original fraction. Any positive proper fraction raised to a power between 0 and 1 will result in a number larger than the original fraction. $\sqrt[4]{\left(\dfrac{3}{4}\right)^3} = \left(\dfrac{3}{4}\right)^{3/4}$, which will be larger than the original fraction of $\dfrac{3}{4}$ because the exponent is between 0 and 1. $\left(\dfrac{3}{4}\right)^{3/4} \approx 0.806$. You will not have to compute the actual value of $\left(\dfrac{3}{4}\right)^{3/4}$, but you should recognize that the result is larger than $\dfrac{3}{4}(= 0.75)$.

11. 25 more games: This is a weighted averages problem. We can set up a table to calculate the number of games he must play to obtain a weighted average win rate of 60%:

Poker Games	First 25 Games	Remaining Games	Total
Wins	$(0.4)25 = 10$	$(0.8)x$	$(0.6)(25 + x)$
Losses			
TOTAL	25	x	$25 + x$

Thus, $10 + 0.8x = (0.6)(25 + x)$ $10 + 0.8x = 15 + 0.6x$ $0.2x = 5$ $x = 25$

12. 60%: This is a weighted averages problem. We can set up a table to calculate the answer, and assume that we purchased 100 lbs. of Brand A:

Pounds (lbs)	Brand A	Brand B	Total
Millet	40	$0.65x$	$(0.5)(100 + x)$
Other stuff	60	$0.35x$	$(0.5)(100 + x)$
Total birdseed	100	x	$100 + x$

Thus, $40 + 0.65x = (0.5)(100 + x)$ $40 + 0.65x = 50 + 0.5x$ $0.15x = 10$ $x = \dfrac{1,000}{15}$

Therefore, Brand A is $\dfrac{100}{100 + \dfrac{1,000}{15}} = \dfrac{100}{\dfrac{1,500}{15} + \dfrac{1,000}{15}} = \dfrac{1,500}{2,500} = 60\%$ of the total.

13. 10%: This is a weighted average "percent change" problem. We can set up a table to calculate the answer, and assume that Jar A contains 200 red jellybeans and 100 yellow jellybeans:

Jellybeans	Jar A	Difference	Jar B
Red	200	+40	$200(1.2) = 240$
Yellow	100	−10	$100(0.9) = 90$
Total Jellybeans	300	+30	$240 + 90 = 330$

Thus, Jar B has 30, or 10%, more jellybeans than Jar A.

14. $\dfrac{11}{18}$: This is a weighted average "percent change" problem. We can set up a table to calculate the answer, and assume that last year, there were 100 Revolutionary voters:

Voters	Last Year	This Year	Total
Revolutionary	100	+10	$100(1.1) = 110$
Status Quo	x	$+0.05x$	$x(1.05) = 1.05x$
Total Voters	$100 + x$	$+0.08(100 + x)$	$110 + 1.05x$

Thus, $100 + x + 0.08(100 + x) = 110 + 1.05x$ $108 + 1.08x = 110 + 1.05x$

$0.03x = 2$ $x = \dfrac{2}{0.03} = \dfrac{200}{3}$

Thus, for every 100 Revolutionary voters last year, there were approximately 67 Status Quo voters. The question, however, asks us to compute the percentage of voters who voted Revolutionary <u>this</u> year. Thus, the number of Revolutionary voters this year is $(100)(110) = 110$, and the number of Status Quo voters

this year is $\dfrac{200}{3}(1.05) = \dfrac{210}{3} = 70$. Therefore, $\dfrac{110}{110 + 70} = \dfrac{110}{180} = \dfrac{11}{18}$ of voters, or approximately 61.1%,

voted Revolutionary this year.

15. To convert a percent that contains a decimal to a fraction, write it over a denominator of 100. Shift the decimal points in the numerator and denominator to eliminate the decimal point in the numerator. Then simplify.

$$0.15\% = \frac{0.15}{100} = \frac{15}{10,000} = \mathbf{\frac{3}{2,000}}$$

$$9.6\% = \frac{9.6}{100} = \frac{96}{1,000} = \mathbf{\frac{12}{125}}$$

16. To convert a percent to a decimal, drop the percent sign and shift the decimal point two places to the left.

$2,000\% = \mathbf{20}$
$0.030\% = \mathbf{0.00030}$

17. To convert a decimal to a percent, shift the decimal point two places to the right.

$36.1456 = \mathbf{3,614.56\%}$
$1 = \mathbf{100\%}$

18. $\dfrac{\mathbf{200}}{\mathbf{3}} \times \mathbf{10^{-2}} < \dfrac{\mathbf{3}}{\mathbf{5}} \div \dfrac{\mathbf{8}}{\mathbf{10}} < \dfrac{\mathbf{0.00751}}{\mathbf{0.01}}$

First, simplify all terms and express them in decimal form:

$$\frac{3}{5} \div \frac{8}{10} = \frac{3}{5} \times \frac{10}{8} = \frac{3}{4} = .75$$

$$\frac{0.00751}{0.01} = \frac{0.751}{1} = 0.751$$

$$\frac{200}{3} \times 10^{-2} = 66.\overline{6} \times 10^{-2} = 0.\overline{6}$$

$$0.\overline{6} < 0.75 < 0.751$$

19. **25%.** The Original ratio is \$2.50/\$500. The New ratio is \$3/\$800. We should compute the percent OF the Original that the New ratio represents. Then we can compute the percent change.

$$\frac{\text{New}}{\text{Original}} = \frac{\dfrac{3}{800}}{\dfrac{2.5}{500}} = \frac{3}{800} \times \frac{500}{2.5} = \frac{3}{8} \times \frac{5}{2.5} = \frac{3}{8} \times \frac{2}{1} = \frac{6}{8} = \frac{3}{4} = 75\%$$

Since the New is 75% of the Original, the Change is 75% − 100% = −25% of the Original. We can drop the negative sign, since the question asks how much the ratio decreased. The correct answer is 25%.

20. $Y \times \left(1 + \dfrac{X}{100}\right)$: For this problem we can use the percent change formula:

$$\text{ORIGINAL} \times \left(1 + \frac{\text{Percent Increase}}{100}\right) = \text{NEW}$$

Here Y is the original number, and X is the percent change; we solve for the new number:

$$Y \times \left(1 + \frac{X}{100}\right) = \text{NEW}$$

21. $\dfrac{100(X-Y)}{Y}$: For this problem we can use the percent change formula:

$$\text{ORIGINAL} \times \left(1 + \frac{\text{Percent Increase}}{100}\right) = \text{NEW}$$

Here Y is the original number, and X is the new number; we solve for the percent:

$$Y \times \left(1 + \frac{\text{Pct}}{100}\right) = X \qquad 1 + \frac{\text{Pct}}{100} = \frac{X}{Y} \qquad \frac{\text{Pct}}{100} = \frac{X-Y}{Y} \qquad \text{Pct} = \frac{100(X-Y)}{Y}$$

22. $\dfrac{10{,}000\,X - 100\,YZ}{YZ}$: For this problem we can use the percent change formula:

$$\text{ORIGINAL} \times \left(1 + \frac{\text{Percent Increase}}{100}\right) = \text{NEW}$$

Here Y percent of Z (which is $\dfrac{YZ}{100}$) is the original number, and X is the new number; we solve for the

percent:

$$\frac{YZ}{100} \times \left(1 + \frac{\text{Pct}}{100}\right) = X \qquad\qquad 1 + \frac{\text{Pct}}{100} = \frac{100\,X}{YZ} \qquad\qquad \frac{\text{Pct}}{100} = \frac{100\,X - YZ}{YZ}$$

$$\text{Pct} = \frac{100(100\,X - YZ)}{YZ} = \frac{10{,}000\,X - 100\,YZ}{YZ}$$

23. To estimate a fraction, we can either change the denominator to a nearby factor of 10, or change either the denominator or numerator to make the fraction easy to reduce. There is no "correct" way to do this, but the closer to the real value, the better.

$\dfrac{12}{37}$:   Either change the denominator to $\dfrac{12}{36} = \dfrac{1}{3} = 0.\overline{3}$, a slight overestimate

(because we reduced the denominator), or to $\dfrac{12}{40} = \dfrac{3}{10} = 0.3$, a slight under-

estimate (because we increased the denominator).

$\dfrac{14}{90}$:   Either change the denominator to $\dfrac{14}{100} = 0.14$, an underestimate (because

we increased the denominator), or $\dfrac{15}{90} = \dfrac{1}{6} = 0.1\overline{6}$, an overestimate

(because we increased the numerator).

$\dfrac{13}{51}$:   Either change the denominator to $\dfrac{13}{52} = \dfrac{1}{4} = 0.25$, an underestimate (because

we increased the denominator), or to $\dfrac{13}{50} = 0.26$, an overestimate (because

we reduced the denominator).

$\dfrac{168}{839}$:   Best is to change the denominator to $\dfrac{168}{840} = \dfrac{21}{105} = \dfrac{1}{5} = 0.2$, a very slight

underestimate (because we increased the denominator). Similarly, you might

switch the fraction to $\dfrac{170}{850} = \dfrac{17}{85} = \dfrac{1}{5} = 0.2$, although because we increased

both the numerator and denominator slightly, it is hard to tell whether this

would be an underestimate or overestimate. If you missed those relation-

ships, you could change the fraction to $\dfrac{168}{800} = 0.21$, a slight overestimate

(because we reduced the denominator).

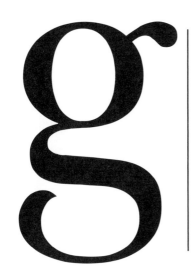

Chapter 8
of

FRACTIONS, DECIMALS, & PERCENTS

OFFICIAL GUIDE PROBLEM SETS: PART II

In This Chapter . . .

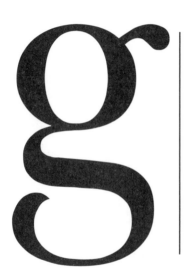

- Fractions, Decimals, & Percents Problem Solving List from *The Official Guides:* PART II
- Fractions, Decimals, & Percents Data Sufficiency List from *The Official Guides:* PART II

Practicing with REAL GMAT Problems

Now that you have completed Part II of FRACTIONS, DECIMALS, & PERCENTS, it is time to test your skills on problems that have actually appeared on real GMAT exams over the past several years.

The problem sets that follow are composed of questions from three books published by the Graduate Management Admission Council® (the organization that develops the official GMAT exam):

The Official Guide for GMAT Review, 12th Edition
The Official Guide for GMAT Quantitative Review
The Official Guide for GMAT Quantitative Review, 2nd Edition
<u>Note</u>: The two editions of the Quant Review book largely overlap. Use one OR the other.

These books contain quantitative questions that have appeared on past official GMAT exams. (The questions contained therein are the property of The Graduate Management Admission Council, which is not affiliated in any way with Manhattan GMAT.)

Although the questions in the Official Guides have been "retired" (they will not appear on future official GMAT exams), they are great practice questions.

In order to help you practice effectively, we have categorized every problem in The Official Guides by topic and subtopic. On the following pages, you will find two categorized lists:

(1) **Problem Solving:** Lists MORE DIFFICULT Problem Solving Fraction, Decimal, & Percent questions contained in *The Official Guides* and categorizes them by subtopic.

(2) **Data Sufficiency:** Lists MORE DIFFICULT Data Sufficiency Fraction, Decimal, & Percent questions contained in *The Official Guides* and categorizes them by subtopic.

Remember that Chapter 6 in Part I of this book contains the first sets of Official Guide problems, which are easier.

Each book in Manhattan GMAT's 8-book strategy series contains its own *Official Guide* lists that pertain to the specific topic of that particular book. If you complete all the practice problems contained on the *Official Guide* lists in each of the 8 Manhattan GMAT strategy books, you will have completed every single question published in *The Official Guides*.

Problem Solving: Part II

from *The Official Guide for GMAT Review, 12th Edition* (pages 20–23 & 152–185), *The Official Guide for GMAT Quantitative Review* (pages 62–85), and *The Official Guide for GMAT Quantitative Review, 2nd Edition* (pages 62–86).

<u>Note</u>: The two editions of the Quant Review book largely overlap. Use one OR the other.

Solve each of the following problems in a notebook, making sure to demonstrate how you arrived at each answer by showing all of your work and computations. If you get stuck on a problem, look back at the FDP strategies and content in this guide to assist you.

<u>Note</u>: Problem numbers preceded by "D" refer to questions in the Diagnostic Test chapter of *The Official Guide for GMAT Review, 12th edition* (pages 20–23).

ADVANCED SET – FRACTIONS, DECIMALS, & PERCENTS

This set picks up from where the General Set in Part I leaves off.

Fractions

> *12th Edition*: 181, 186, 225
> *Quantitative Review*: 154, 162, 165, 167, 176 OR *2nd Edition*: 165, 167, 176

Digits and Decimals

> *12th Edition*: 108, 190, 203, 211, 226
> *Quantitative Review*: 142, 174 OR *2nd Edition*: 174

Percents

> *12th Edition*: 156, 166, 193, 223
> *Quantitative Review*: 138, 143, 156, 158, 159

Successive Percents and Percent Change

> *12th Edition*: 151, 220
> *Quantitative Review*: 100
> OR *2nd Edition*: 100, 154, 155

FDPs

> *12th Edition*: 187

CHALLENGE SHORT SET – FRACTIONS, DECIMALS, & PERCENTS

This set covers Fractions, Decimals, & Percent problems from each of the content areas, including both easier and harder problems, but with a focus on harder problems. The Challenge Short Set duplicates problems from the General Set (in Part I) and the Advanced Set above.

> *12th Edition*: 43, 79, 108, 109, 115, 131, 138, 143, 156, 166, 176, 211, 220, 223, D11, D12
> *Quantitative Review*: 33, 37, 41, 73, 79, 100, 101, 120, 134, 142, 143, 159, 165, 167
> OR *2nd Edition*: 35, 39, 61, 69, 100, 101, 120, 134, 143, 154, 155, 159, 165, 167

Data Sufficiency: Part II

from *The Official Guide for GMAT Review, 12ᵗʰ Edition* (pages 24–26 & 272–288), *The Official Guide for GMAT Quantitative Review* (pages 149–157), and *The Official Guide for GMAT Quantitative Review, 2nd Edition* (pages 152–163).

<u>Note</u>: The two editions of the Quant Review book largely overlap. Use one OR the other.

Solve each of the following problems in a notebook, making sure to demonstrate how you arrived at each answer by showing all of your work and computations. If you get stuck on a problem, look back at the FDP strategies and content contained in this guide to assist you.

Practice REPHRASING both the questions and the statements by using variables and constructing equations. The majority of data sufficiency problems can be rephrased; however, if you have difficulty rephrasing a problem, try testing numbers to solve it. It is especially important that you familiarize yourself with the directions for data sufficiency problems, and that you memorize the 5 fixed answer choices that accompany all data sufficiency problems.

<u>Note</u>: Problem numbers preceded by "D" refer to questions in the Diagnostic Test chapter of *The Official Guide for GMAT Review, 12ᵗʰ edition* (pages 24–26).

ADVANCED SET – FRACTIONS, DECIMALS, & PERCENTS

This set picks up from where the General Set in Part I leaves off.

Fractions
> *12ᵗʰ Edition*: 113
> *Quantitative Review*: 113 OR *2nd Edition*: 119

Digits and Decimals
> *12ᵗʰ Edition*: 110, 151, 167, D25
> *QR 2nd Edition*: 96, 102, 104

Percents
> *12ᵗʰ Edition*: 88, 92, 142

Successive Percents and Percent Change
> *12ᵗʰ Edition*: 120

FDPs
> *12ᵗʰ Edition*: 139, 143

CHALLENGE SHORT SET – FRACTIONS, DECIMALS, & PERCENTS

This set covers Fractions, Decimals, & Percent problems from each of the content areas, including both easier and harder problems, but with a focus on harder problems. The Challenge Short Set duplicates problems from the General Set (in Part I) and the Advanced Set above.
> *12ᵗʰ Edition*: 27, 52, 61, 79, 88, 113, 120, 142, 143, 151, 167, D25
> *Quantitative Review*: 5, 22, 48, 49, 72, 113
> OR *2nd Edition*: 5, 49, 50, 75, 96, 119

mba Mission

Every candidate has a unique story to tell.

We have the creative experience to help you tell yours.

We are **mbaMission**, published authors with elite MBA experience who will work with you one-on-one to craft complete applications that will force the admissions committees to take notice. Benefit from straightforward guidance and personal mentorship as you define your unique attributes and reveal them to the admissions committees via a story only you can tell.

We will guide you through our "Complete Start to Finish Process":

- ☑ Candidate assessment, application strategy and program selection
- ☑ Brainstorming and selection of essay topics
- ☑ Outlining and essay structuring
- ☑ Unlimited essay editing
- ☑ Letter of recommendation advice
- ☑ Resume construction and review
- ☑ Interview preparation, mock interviews and feedback
- ☑ Post-acceptance and scholarship counseling

Monday Morning Essay Tip: Overrepresenting Your Overrepresentation

Many in the MBA application pool—particularly male investment bankers—worry that they are overrepresented. While you cannot change your work history, you can change the way you introduce yourself to admissions committees. Consider the following examples:

Example 1: "As an investment banking analyst at Bank of America, I am responsible for creating Excel models...."
Example 2: "At 5:30 pm, I could rest easy. The deadline for all other offers had passed. At that point, I knew...."

In the first example, the candidate starts off by mistakenly introducing the reader to the very over-representation that he/she should be trying to avoid emphasizing. In the second example, the banker immerses the reader in an unraveling mystery. This keeps the reader intrigued and focused on the applicant's story and actions rather than making the specific job title and responsibilities the center of the text. While each applicant's personal situation is different, every candidate can approach his/her story so as to mitigate the effects of overrepresentation.

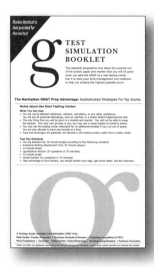